The Seventh Learning College Principle

A Framework for Transformational Change

Edited by
Dr. Alicia B. Harvey-Smith

NASPA
Student Affairs Administrators
in Higher Education

Additional copies may be purchased by contacting the NASPA publications department
at 301-638-1749 or visiting http://www.naspa.org/publications.

ISBN 0-931654-37-8

DEDICATION

This book is dedicated to learners past, present, and future and to those who seek authentic transformation on their behalf.

ACKNOWLEDGEMENTS

Alicia B. Harvey-Smith

There were many who inspired this work, and the authors and I wish to thank them all. There is only space to name a few, so what follows is an incomplete mentioning of individuals and institutions to whom we are grateful.

This work would not have been possible without the involvement of the institutions that were examined as part of the initial research on my dissertation. Thank you for the lessons learned and your dedication to creating powerful learning environments for our students and for sharing your learning journeys and institutions.

The other authors and I acknowledge each of our own institutions and organizations and those contacted as a result of researching the themes that appear in these pages. Your support helped shape this work.

We also acknowledge the groundbreaking work of Terry O'Banion, who graciously wrote the foreword for this publication; John Tagg, Robert Barr, and George Boggs for unveiling the learning paradigm and its principles and possibilities; and the work of Everett Rogers, whose diffusion of innovations framework provided a new lens with which to examine innovation and change in student affairs.

I wish to acknowledge my husband, Donald, for his continuous support and encouragement and each author who contributed time and talent to this work and raised the bar of my understanding of this emerging paradigm. I also acknowledge the Learning and Student Development Division, Community College of Baltimore County, Catonsville campus, for ongoing commitment to transforming its community of learners. Thanks also to the National Association of Student Personnel Administrators, Gwendolyn Jordan Dungy, and Kevin Kruger for seeing the value of this work to the student affairs profession and its broader applicability and potential influence on organizational transformation and positive change sustainability.

TABLE OF CONTENTS

ABOUT THE AUTHORS

Dr. Jack Becherer is president of Rock Valley College in Rockford, Illinois.. The majority of his career has been devoted to working in student development at community colleges. His initial position was as a counselor at Thomas Nelson Community College in Virginia, followed by counseling, teaching psychology and communications, and directing assessment efforts at St. Louis Community College. He served as the vice president of student development at Moraine Valley Community College in Palos Hills, Illinois. Dr. Becherer has been a frequent speaker and writer in student development.

Dr. Sharon Fries-Britt is an associate professor in the College of Education at the University of Maryland, College Park. She earned a Ph.D. and an undergraduate degree from the University of Maryland, College Park, and an M.A. in college student personnel from Ohio State University. Her research focuses on high-achieving Black collegians and their academic, social, and psychological experiences. Prior to her academic appointment, she served for 12 years as an administrator in higher education. She has been an independent consultant for more than 20 years.

Danette S. Gerald is a summa cum laude graduate of Howard University and received her master's degree in administration, planning, and social policy from the Harvard University Graduate School of Education. She is currently a doctoral student in the higher education program at the University of Maryland, and her research interests focus on diverse learning environments and postsecondary access for low-income students.

Rashida Govan is the director of student life at the Community College of Baltimore County, Essex. She earned her M.Ed. in counseling and personnel services from the University of Maryland and her B.S. in elementary education from Morgan State University. Her research interests focus on access, achievement, and retention issues for African American women and other underrepresented students in higher education. Govan is also committed to diversity education and training and has presented on topics ranging from intercultural communication to racial identity development.

Dr. Alicia B. Harvey-Smith is dean of learning and student development at the Community College of Baltimore County. She earned a Ph.D. from the University of Maryland, College Park, in college student personnel, an M.S.Ed. from Johns Hopkins University in counseling and guidance, and a B.S. from Morgan State University in business administration. She served on boards for the National Council for Student Development , the Council for the Advancement of Standards in Higher Education, and the American Association of Community Colleges' Commission on Academic, Student and Community Development. She is the author of *A Framework for Transforming Learning Organizations: Proposing a New Learning College Principle* (2003) and *Getting Real: Proven Strategies for Student Survival and Academic Success* (1998).

Ted James is dean of student development at Douglas College, a large community college in Vancouver, British Columbia, Canada. He has served as a Canadian representative on the board of the National Council on Student Development and as coordinator of regional representatives. He has also served as a board member for the Canadian Association of College and Student Services. Author of *Learner Support and Success: Determining the educational support needs for learners into the 21st century* (1999), he is a keen observer of the evolving future of student services.

Dr. Susan Komives is associate professor, college student personnel, at the University of Maryland, College Park. She received her Ed.D. from the University of Tennessee at Knoxville in education administration and supervision. Her research interests include student leadership development, higher education futures issues and trends, and administrative leadership.

Her teaching interests include organizational change and leadership of student affairs programs. Dr. Komives is a noted author and lecturer.

Zakiya S. Lee is a third-year doctoral student in college student personnel administration at the University of Maryland, College Park. She earned a B.S. in elementary education and B.A. in psychology, also from the University of Maryland, and an M.A. in higher education and student affairs from Ohio State University. Lee served as the coordinator of Greek life at Ohio State and a teacher in Baltimore public schools. Her research interests include college choice and access issues for students from urban school systems.

Dr. Rufus Sylvester Lynch is dean of the Whitney M. Young Jr. School of Social Work at Clark Atlanta University. He is also president and principal investigator of the Institute for the Advancement of Working Families. He earned a doctorate in social work from the University of Pennsylvania, a master's degree in social work from the University of Pittsburgh, and a B.A. in sociology from Morgan State University.

Dr. Hanne Mawhinney is an associate professor and graduate program coordinator for organizational leadership and policy studies at the University of Maryland, College Park. She received her B.A. from Simon Fraser University, British Columbia, and her M.A. and Ph.D. in educational administration from the University of Ottawa. Her research focuses on the institutional dynamics of change in educational organizations. Dr. Mawhinney is a member of the editorial boards of *Educational Administration Quarterly*, *The American Educational Research Journal*, and *School Leadership and Management*.

Dr. Jacquelyn Mitchell, J.D., LCISW, is a member of the graduate faculty of the Jackson State University School of Social Work. An educator, attorney, forensic social worker, and mediator; she has held several academic appointments and senior positions in federal and state government, practiced law in the public and private sectors, and consulted for nonprofit and for-profit entities on legal, management, and social service issues. She has published several professional manuscripts and regularly makes juried and invited presentations at transdisciplinary national, regional, and local professional meetings.

Dr. Vincent Mumford is a professor in the College of Education at the University of Central Florida. He serves as coordinator of the Sports Leadership Program and specializes in sports administration and leadership. He received his doctoral degree in educational leadership from the University of Delaware, where he studied as a Holmes Scholar. Dr. Mumford has a diverse professional background, with experience in academics, administration, and athletics as a participant, teacher, coach, and administrator.

Dr. Terry O'Banion is president emeritus and senior league fellow at the League for Innovation in the Community College and director of the Community College Leadership Program for Walden University. During his 42 years in the community college, he has consulted in more than 800 community colleges and universities, has written 12 books and more than 125 articles, and has been honored with three national awards established in his name. His 1997 book, *A Learning College for the 21st Century*, has influenced colleges worldwide to become more learning-centered institutions.

Dr. Kim Poast is the dean of students at the Community College of Denver. She has worked in the field of higher education for 17 years and specializes in leadership development, cultural/gender implications of student development theory, first-generation students, and feminist theory. She earned a Ph.D. from the University of Northern Colorado in higher education student affairs leadership and a master's degree from California Lutheran University. She is a member of the National Council on Student Development and the National Association of Student Personnel Administrators.

Dr. Joyce Romano is vice president for student affairs at Valencia Community College in Orlando, Fla. She has 26 years of experience in student services. Her work at Valencia has focused on designing and implementing LifeMap, a developmental advising system; Atlas, an online portal learning community; and the redesign of student services. Dr. Romano has a B.A. in psychology from Central Washington College at Cortland, an M.S. in counseling psychology from Central Washington University, and an Ed.D. in higher education from the University of Kansas.

Mary Jean Rusnak is an academic adviser at the Community College of Baltimore County. She earned her graduate degree in clinical community counseling from Johns Hopkins University and an undergraduate degree from the College of Notre Dame in Maryland. She was formerly a counselor for the House of Ruth, a nonprofit agency that provides services for victims of domestic violence. Her education directly relates to her passion for service and reflects her commitment to assisting people from all walks of life to achieve their personal and educational goals.

Dr. Sanford C. Shugart is president of Valencia Community College in Orlando, Fla.. Prior to being at Valencia, Dr. Shugart served some eight years as president of North Harris College, a large community college in north Houston. There he led efforts in advanced technology, student success, an extensive construction agenda, and aggressive outreach to the inner city. Dr. Shugart earned his bachelor of science, master of arts in teaching, and Ph.D. at the University of North Carolina, Chapel Hill. He is widely known for his speaking and writing on servant leadership and is a published poet and songwriter.

FOREWORD

Terry O'Banion

In the last decade of the 20th century, educators across the country came face-to-face with a stark reality: All their efforts at making substantive reforms in the educational enterprise—involving billions of dollars, new regulations, new standards, new programs, new practices—had failed. The little red schoolhouse that Carnegie had built was not made of bricks; it was made of sticks and straw and had been crumbling for decades. One critic of school reform (Leonard, 1992) suggested, "We can no longer improve the education of our children by improving school as we know it. The time has come to recognize that school is not the solution. It is the problem" (p. 26).

What went wrong has been well documented (Perelman, 1992; Wingspread Group on Higher Education, 1993; O'Banion, 1997). The review of key national reports in the first chapter of this book documents the failure of reform in detail. In a nutshell, educational leaders continued to prop up the little red schoolhouse that Carnegie had built by bolting on new programs and practices to an outdated architecture. Initially, even information technology supported the traditional architecture of education. Faculties at the beginning of the new millennium were still using the new technology primarily to improve overheads for their lectures; technology had great potential to expand really bad teaching.

The challenge to bring about change was formidable. "Higher education is a thousand years of tradition wrapped in a hundred years of bureaucracy" (R. Moe, as cited in Armajani, B., et al., 1994, p. 1). Tweaking a broken system by adding a new innovation did not produce substantive change. The inherited architecture of education was time-bound, place-bound, efficiency-bound, and role-bound. A new way of thinking about the entire educational enterprise was needed, and the Wingspread Group on Higher Education issued the call: "Putting learning at the heart of the academic enterprise will mean overhauling the conceptual, procedural, curricular, and other architecture of postsecondary education on most campuses" (1993, p. 14). This clear and simple statement echoed an emerging vision for the future: The Learning Revolution places learning first by overhauling the traditional architecture of education.

This was radical change, change that required major transformation. A new learning paradigm—first championed by George Boggs, Robert Barr, and John Tagg at Palomar College in California—helped pave the way, and an idea encapsulated in the learning college—which I proposed in 1997—suggested a framework and a plan for institutional transformation.

In this book, Alicia Harvey-Smith and her colleagues have examined the nooks and crannies of the change process and of the field of student affairs in terms of the impact of the learning college idea and its six principles — one of the first national efforts to do so. Drawing on her recent research at the University of Maryland, College Park, Harvey-Smith has even created a "seventh principle" of the learning college: Create and nurture an organizational culture that is open and responsive to change and learning. Harvey-Smith's principle transcends the six principles of the original learning college idea, bringing an organizing focus that adds heft and ballast to the evolving concepts. As a result, I am pleased to endorse the seventh learning college principle as a significant contribution to the concept of the learning college and encourage its adoption, as it has tremendous implications for transformation in learning organizations.

Furthermore, she has engaged a formidable group of colleagues to join her creative journey in exploring and teasing out the substantive connections and opportunities between the learning college and student affairs. Ted James got it exactly right in Chapter 2 when he said, "This chapter then explores how the learning college concept is easily assimilated by, and closely compatible to, the work of student affairs because it aligns with the traditional values and philosophy of student affairs, because reaction to the inadequacies of the instruction paradigm has been a common theme in the evolution of student affairs, and because the changing personnel roles needed to operate a learning college harmonize well with the various skills and expertise of student affairs professionals."

It is no surprise to my colleagues of the '60s and '70s that there is considerable compatibility between the learning college and student affairs. I cut my teeth on the profession of student affairs beginning in 1960 as a dean of students at Central Florida Community College. My master's degree was in counseling psychology at the University of Florida under the tutelage of Arthur C. Combs, with whom I completed all the doctoral work to become a psychotherapist. I once had dinner at Combs' home with Carl Rogers—just the three of us—and on another occasion with Abraham Maslow—again, just the three of us; Combs saw more potential in me than I realized at the time! I was deeply steeped in client-centered therapy and Maslow's hierarchy of needs and embraced humanistic education with the fiery passion of a true believer. My first book was *The Shared Journey: An Introduction to Encounter* that was once used in over 200 colleges and universities as a student text. Later, my interest in psychotherapy morphed into the administration of student affairs (the impact of operating as a dean of students), and I joined Melvene Hardee at Florida State University for a Ph.D. in higher education administration and a thorough immersion in the world of student affairs. Beginning in 1966, I wrote over 40 articles, chapters, and monographs on student affairs; my book with Alice Thurston—*Student Development Programs in Community Junior Colleges*—was published by Prentice-Hall in 1971 and proposed "an emerging model" of student affairs for the community college. That "emerging model" of student affairs contained the seeds that would later sprout into the learning college.

I always thought that student affairs could find a comfortable and substantive home in the learning college, and the careful reader will see the significant role student affairs can play in that model. But readers of *A Learning College for the 21st Century* will find few, if any references to "student affairs," or "student personnel work," or even "counselors" in the text. Hopefully, I was also able to avoid the use of such terms as "professor," "teacher," and "instructor" (although these terms are so embedded in the old architecture of education that I am sure I used them on occasion). My goal was to think in new ways about our roles as educators, and I adopted a term Carl Rogers first used—learning facilitators. I wanted to make the point that all of us in the college are facilitators of learning, and that the old divisions are artifacts of an outdated architecture. We build our own silos in student affairs when we use language that separates—as do our colleagues in academic and financial affairs—and I found it helpful to be more inclusive by emphasizing that everyone in the institution plays an important role in helping students to expand and improve their learning.

Whatever terms the professionals in student affairs use to designate their presence in the institution, they may play the most significant roles of all in helping students succeed. They are there at the beginning steps of admission, orientation, registration; they are there throughout the continuing processes of advising, counseling, assessment, mentoring, student activities, career development; they are there to support and intervene and redirect when students flounder in the classrooms; they are there for faculty every day; and they are there after the students leave to follow up, recommend, articulate, and welcome home. In all of these functions of student affairs and others not listed here, student affairs professionals have an opportunity to become full and respected partners in the educational enterprise if they will keep their eye on "learning" as the primary goal, the all-encompassing mission and philosophy, and the ultimate outcome of their very important work.

In her own good work represented in this book and in her career, Alicia Harvey-Smith has extended our knowledge and practice of student affairs to new levels of opportunity that will prove to be of enormous value to our students if we will but heed her call for transformation and action.

REFERENCES

Armajani, B., et al. (1994). *A model for the reinvented higher education system: State policy and college learning.* Denver, CO: Education Commission of the States.

Leonard, G. (1992, May). The end of school. *The Atlantic, 269*(5).

O'Banion, T. (1997). *A learning college for the 21st century.* Phoenix, AZ: Oryx Press.

Perelman, L. J. (1992). *School's out: A radical new formula for the revitalization of America's educational system.* New York: Avon Books.

Wingspread Group on Higher Education. (1993). *An American imperative: Higher expectations for higher education.* Racine, WI: The Johnson Foundation.

PREFACE

Alicia B. Harvey-Smith

In 1997, the American Council on Education and the American Association of Community Colleges published Terry O'Banion's *A Learning College for the 21st Century*, a seminal work that captured the essence of an emerging learning revolution and new learning paradigm in higher education. The key message of O'Banion's book is straightforward: Every college should place learning as its highest priority in every policy, program, practice, and the way it uses personnel. Six principles in the book can guide colleges in achieving this goal:

The book is now in its fourth printing, and in 1998 it won the Phillip E. Frandson Award for Literature from the University Continuing Education Association. The book has had considerable impact on education; conferences on the Learning College have been held in Japan, Australia, the Netherlands, Singapore, Scotland, and the United Arab Emirates. Twenty-one related dissertations have been published to date.

O'Banion did not stop at writing a significant book. As president of the League for Innovation in the Community College, he championed the learning college and made it part of the action agenda for the league. He wrote three monographs and dozens of articles on the learning college, created a series of learning abstracts, integrated a focus on learning into league national conferences, and consulted in more than a hundred colleges and universities on the learning college. Most important, he and his colleagues at the league secured a grant of more than $1 million from Atlantic Philanthropic to create the Learning College Project, which involved 12 community colleges that worked together to become more learning-centered institutions. In addition, he and his colleagues secured another grant of more than $1 million from Pew Charitable Trusts to establish models of learning outcomes with 16 community colleges. The results of these projects have been very influential on other community colleges and can be reviewed on the league's Website at http://www.league.org.

The Community College of Baltimore County (CCBC) was one of the 12 Vanguard Learning Colleges. Thus, as the dean of learning and student development there, I participated in the Learning College Project. Through my work in the project and by reading O'Banion's book and related literature, I came to see the connections between the learning college idea and student affairs. I decided to work on a dissertation that would explore this connection in depth.

In the spring of 2003, I completed my journey to the doctorate, with a dissertation entitled "The Adoption of the Learning Paradigm in Student Affairs Divisions in Vanguard Community Colleges: A Case Analysis." This journey ignited a passion for inquiry for the purpose of providing "real solutions" to the critical challenges of change and determining new frameworks for sustainability. As a result, I have created a seventh learning college principle—endorsed by O'Banion and other leaders—as a contribution to the concept of the learning college. That principle provides the framework for this book.

The seventh learning college principle—create and nurture an organizational culture that is both open and responsive to change and learning—may represent the next step in a logical progression to improve understanding of how institutional environments may be transformed to support the learning paradigm. The book provides the reader an opportunity to extend transformational learning and addresses the critical role that student affairs divisions can play in learning organizations. Sixteen other authors contributed to this book, and each brings a unique and valuable perspective to this phenomenon.

The learning college transformation is one of the most influential educational reform movements taking shape in postsecondary education in the 21st century. As institutions redefine themselves to focus more on student learning, how can student affairs and other organizations become more learning-centered? *The Seventh Learning College Principle: A Framework for Transformational Change* is one of the first resources to address this paradigm shift through the lens of student affairs. It is offered as a blueprint for organizations wanting to learn more about adopting the learning paradigm and creating environmental cultures that support the growth of learners.

The book is written to expand readers' understanding of change and the processes necessary to bring organizations into alignment with this emerging paradigm. It includes both theory and practice. It provides an overview of educational reform and educational change models, an analysis of the evolving role of student affairs in the reform movement, and strategies for aligning student affairs practice with learning principles and building a culture of evidence through assessment.

This book examines how to achieve the diffusion of the learning paradigm in student affairs and other complex environments and how institutional influences can support or hinder transformation in social systems. It also provides learning-centered frameworks for change and introduces the seventh learning college principle into the discourse for broader discussion. This book additionally provides a rationale for moving the level of student affairs' involvement from the edge to the center of leadership and supports strategically reducing boundaries that are remnants of a traditional educational system and transcending structures that repress the ability to activate the seventh learning college principle.

CHAPTER 1

Clarion Calls for Reform and Change in Postsecondary Education

Sharon Fries-Britt, Danette S. Gerald, and Zakiya S. Lee

"Everything is changing all the time: Individuals, systems, environments, the rules, and the processes of evolution."

—MARGARET WHEATLEY AND KELLNER-ROGERS

INTRODUCTION

The landscape of higher education has changed significantly since the first American universities were founded nearly 400 years ago. In the 20th century, colleges and universities sought to broaden access to higher education, improve teaching and learning, diversify faculty and administrators, contain costs, and embrace emerging technologies. The 21st century saw a continuation of these issues and ushered in an era of expanding higher education through technology (Trow, 2001). Many of these changes have made colleges and universities vastly different than they were even 10 years ago.

Some argue that the growth of postsecondary education has been necessary to meet the demands of an increasingly diverse and multifaceted society (Rendon & Hope, 1996) in which educational access and mastery of academic skills remain prerequisites to professional careers (College Board, 1999) and the pursuit of democratic ideals. Few would disagree that higher education is important. However, the debate often centers on the role higher education should play in an increasingly complex society.

This chapter focuses on several calls for reform and change in higher education at the close of the 20th century and the dawn of the 21st. The chapter starts by identifying key organizations and professional associations that have called for change in postsecondary education. The important role that many of these organizations have in setting the national and local agenda in education cannot be underestimated. Their calls for change have been instrumental in directing the initiatives and programs designed at the campus level to serve students, faculty, and staff. Many of these organizations provide guidelines and principles that govern the professional behavior and commitments of individuals in the field of education.

The second section examines the calls for change from individual scholars. We identify five themes/calls for change that cut across the literature and reflect the work of many scholars. The final theme calls for change that affects students and their learning. This theme sets the context for this book. Understanding the factors that enhance learning experiences for students is fundamental to the purpose and success of higher education. The chapter ends with observations about the challenges facing postsecondary education in a rapidly changing society.

ORGANIZATIONAL CALLS FOR CHANGE

Wingspread Group on Higher Education

One of the broadest calls for change at the end of the 20th century came from the Wingspread Group on Higher Education, which recognized "a disturbing and dangerous mismatch" (1993, p. 1) between what America needs from higher education and what America is receiving from higher education. In a report entitled "An American Imperative: Higher Expectations for Higher Education," the Wingspread Group expressed concern about the future of education and, consequently, the future of the United States. It maintained that while the rate of change in society has increased greatly, the goals and organizational functioning of colleges and universities are often outdated. The Wingspread Group called for expanded access to education, arguing that more people need to be educated at higher levels.

The Wingspread Group recognized that proposing change for over 3,000 colleges and universities is a daunting task, considering the amount of variance and diversity among institutions. Although colleges and universities certainly have different procedures to initiate change, the group identified three common issues: taking values seriously, putting student learning first, and creating a nation of leaders.

Universities that take values seriously focus on liberal education. A liberal education is at the center of the development of social and personal values. When values are seriously considered, campuses will model those values and offer students opportunities to reflect on society. By putting student learning first, institutions shift focus from the concerns and needs of educators to the needs of students. This shift results in campuses setting higher expectations for students and improving the resources that help students meet those expectations.

Finally, in an effort to create a nation of leaders, colleges and universities must broaden their thinking about education to include preschool through postgraduate work. This increased attention to the renewal of K-12 and postsecondary education includes establishing clear standards for matriculation and degree completion, creating clear definitions for what students at each level of education should know and be able to do, and preparing and recruiting more effective teachers at all levels.

National Association of Student Personnel Administrators

In 1995, the National Association of Student Personnel Administrators (NASPA) published *Reasonable Expectations: Renewing the Educational Compact Between Institutions and Students*. In this document, NASPA identified change that was occurring in higher education due to the shifting demographics of college students, increased demand for participation in higher education, and pressure from external forces. These forces affect the relationship between the student and the institution. As institutions are pressured to be responsive to change, the quality of undergraduate education is not given the highest priority. Kuh, Miller, Lyons, and Trow (1995) identified expectations that students and institutions can have of one another. These expectations were designed to improve learning productivity.

Kuh et al. (1995) divided these "reasonable expectations" into the following areas: teaching and learning, the curriculum, institutional integrity, the quality of institutional life, and educational services. In each domain, the authors noted what students and faculty can expect from each other as the institution works to transform undergraduate education. The following examples represent changes in expectations that are intended to increase student success.

Concerning teaching and learning, students should expect teachers to be knowledgeable and available; institutions should acknowledge human differences and help students make out-of-class connections; institutions should expect their students to prepare for and attend class. As a way to shift the curriculum, institutions must have advisers available to students and periodically review the curriculum; students should seek advice from faculty and monitor their progress toward completion of the requirements of their program.

Institutions that operate with integrity should be good models of moral and ethical behavior; the institution should encourage academic integrity; students should be familiar with what ethical behavior and academic integrity mean and should challenge violations by peers or institutional leaders. Changes to the quality of institutional life would lead students to expect their college or university to support diversity across campus and to provide a harassment-free living and learning environment; institutions should support connections between themselves, students, and the community and should expect that students contribute to making improvements in the quality of institutional life; students are expected to participate in community events and institutional governance. Finally, expectations about the educational services of a college or university include providing services by skilled experts; making sure students are informed and responsible users of campus services; and assessing student needs and the extent to which services are used. A recent publication, *Learning Reconsidered: A Campus-Wide Focus on the Student Experience* (American College Personnel Association & National Association of Student Personnel Administrators, 2004) focuses on the importance of the integration of academics with personal achievement, a well as the absolute need for accountability through strong learning outcomes measures.

Kellogg Commission on the Future of State and Land-Grant Universities

In 1997, the National Association of State Universities and Land-Grant Colleges (NASULGC), with the support of the W. K. Kellogg Foundation, began releasing the recommendations of a national commission that was charged with rethinking the responsibility of public higher education. The "Returning to Our Roots" series includes reports that provide guidance to public colleges and universities as they work to create change on their campuses.

In the report on "The Student Experience," the commission recommended that institutions return to their roots by reviving the reason state and land-grant institutions were established—"to put students first" (p. 11). It challenged institutions to become genuine, supportive, and inspiring learning communities. It posited that learning communities must be centered on students, and that the community must be a healthy environment for learners. In the "Student Access" report, the commission expressed concern for ensuring that students are able to attend state and land-grant institutions and to complete their degree. In order to achieve more access, institutions must focus on academic preparation, admissions policies, support services, and institutional flexibility. The increased access that is sought, the commission contended, is not only to higher education but to "the full promise of American life" (p. 17).

The report on the "Engaged Institution" presented methods by which universities and colleges can change in response to the public's perception that higher education is unresponsive, out of touch, and outdated. Engaged institutions are responsive to the communities served, academically neutral, and accessible to potential partners. They integrate the teaching and service mission with institutional scholarship goals, coordination, and resource partnerships; show respect for partners; and make an effort to create academic-community partnerships.

"A Learning Society" advanced the idea of creating an environment that engages in lifelong learning-a "learning society" (p. 29). The report recommended that public institutions make lifelong learning a central part of their mission by increasing the number of learning opportunities, cultivating partnerships, creating learning environments that focus on improving reasoning skills and faculty development, and providing public support for lifelong learning. Finally, the report on "Coherent Campus Culture" expressed the goal of improving connections among departments and units that have become increasingly fragmented.

American Association for Higher Education, American College Personnel Association, and National Association of Student Personnel Administrators

In 1998, three professional associations joined forces to write a report outlining the importance of collaboration in colleges and universities. "Powerful Partnerships: A Shared Responsibility for Learning" was written by the Joint Task Force on Student Learning, comprising members of the American Association for Higher Education (AAHE), the American College Personnel Association (ACPA), and the National Association of Student Personnel Administrators (NASPA) (1998).

This report emphasized that improvements to higher education will be most successful when all forces on campus-especially academic affairs and student affairs-combine to marshal these changes. The task force contended that changes are necessary if we are to properly equip students for the challenges they will face in life.

The task force identified 10 learning principles to outline ways to improve learning:

1. Creating learning environments and experiences in which students can make and sustain connections
2. Providing students with compelling situations that magnify the learning process
3. Encouraging active participation by the learner
4. Educating in a holistic manner

5. Supporting the social nature of learning through cooperation
6. Establishing a positive educational climate
7. Providing feedback
8. Facilitating informal learning experiences
9. Being able to broadly apply skills and knowledge
10. Monitoring one's own learning

"Powerful Partnerships" provided descriptions of programs and efforts at many colleges and universities that address each of the 10 principles. These exemplary practices demonstrate the possibilities that exist when professionals, especially those in student and academic affairs, collaborate to improve the quality of student learning. The task force contended that everyone on campus is responsible for enhancing learning.

American Council on Education

The American Council on Education (ACE) has also recognized the need for change in American higher education. It produced a series of occasional papers entitled "On Change" (1998-2001). The series includes documents that provide colleges and universities with reports from transforming institutions, information on change for governing boards, and a primer on taking charge of institutional change.

In the first document of this series, "En Route to Transformation," ACE proposed that traditional higher education must be overhauled if it is to compete with more convenient, less costly forms of education (e.g., distance education, corporate universities, and transnational delivery). As other organizations have noted, affordability, educational and financial accountability, increased demand for high-quality education and excellent teaching, changing student demographics, and the impact of technology are some of the challenges that institutions of higher education face. ACE's call is for transformational change, or change that alters underlying assumptions and behaviors of the institution, affects the entire institution, and is enduring. According to ACE, putting learning first, linking institutions to their communities, and making postsecondary education more affordable and cost-effective are the arenas in which change can be made.

W.K. Kellogg Foundation

In 2000, the W.K. Kellogg Foundation produced *Leadership Reconsidered: Engaging Higher Education in Social Change* (Astin & Astin, 2000). The authors maintained that change is necessary in order for institutions of higher learning to produce more effective leaders. They called for the "rethinking of leadership practices in higher education" (Kellogg, 2000, p. viii). The onus was placed on higher education because of its major role in influencing the quality of leadership in America. Colleges and universities indirectly have a hand in the precollegiate development of all citizens through the establishment of standards and training for the country's educators. The authors believed that focusing on leadership and leadership development in postsecondary education would enhance the job of postsecondary education in shaping the future of the country. Change, however, is not strictly the responsibility of the institution but also that of faculty, administrators, and students.

The change envisioned by Kellogg benefits all of society but is funneled through those who will be the leaders of society. Since faculty and student affairs professionals tend to have the most interactions with students, they are a critical part of the change process. Moreover, these individuals enjoy influence among their peers and administrative staff. They have the potential to reach many entities on campus. Accordingly, they are called to be leaders and to enact change in their roles as teachers, scholars, and servants to the institution.

The Kellogg Foundation also called on college and university presidents (or CEOs) to be leaders of institutional change. The presidents' role is significant because of the variety of constituencies over whom they have influence. The authors posited that CEOs who effect change will be role models for those with whom they work most closely. Ideally, this would begin a snowball effect of change for the entire institution.

Association of American Colleges and Universities

The Association of American Colleges and Universities' (AAC&U) "Greater Expectations" (2002) acknowledged that higher education faces many challenges in society. The national panel that was assembled stated, "...the enormity and congruence of the current challenges require a radical rethinking of what we should expect from, and how we should provide, college education" (AAC&U, 2002, p. iv). Although many students begin and complete college, there are still many who are not retained or receive degrees despite being unprepared for life after college. This document requested a transformative, powerful, high-quality education for all who aspire to attend. The panel called for "greater expectations" for student achievement that must be integrated into institutions of higher learning if citizens are to be productive in ever-changing workplaces.

To achieve these goals, the panel recommended that the focus of a college education be learning and accomplishment. Student learning would be at the center of the decision-making process. Teachers would employ techniques that engage students in the learning process, set higher expectations, implement learning-centered practices, and inform the public of this reinvigorated style.

Several themes cut across the organizational calls for change. First, institutions must be willing to recommit to students. Putting students first is essential to the work of higher education. Second, a focus on students requires that more effort be put into collaboration. The call for collaboration is essential in a time of scarce resources and increasing responsibilities. Collaboration must occur at the campus level, across institutional types, with the federal government and private industry. Third, many organizations have said that higher education is outdated and no longer in touch with the needs of society. Other themes center on the improvement of teaching and learning and having greater expectations of teachers and students.

The climate of intense change can be overwhelming for higher education institutions. Kuh et al. (1995) acknowledged that creating change is challenging. The goal of improved undergraduate education, however, is too critical to ignore. It is important to set manageable expectations so that individuals can make a difference in the process. Institutions must recognize the transformative nature of higher education and plan a change process with clearer expectations and norms than currently exist.

INDIVIDUAL SCHOLARS' CALL FOR CHANGE

In this era of great technological advances and changing student demographics, higher education advocates and critics alike assert that American universities are in the midst of an identity crisis. Several scholars have identified key challenges to which postsecondary institutions must respond if they are to effectively educate future generations of students. Five themes consistently emerge from the literature: 1) changing purpose of higher education, 2) changing student demographics, 3) access and the rising cost of higher education, 4) the impact of technology, and 5) students and their learning.

Changing Purpose of Higher Education

Throughout the first half of the 20th century, higher education trained the ruling strata for positions of leadership that would allow them to maintain their status as members of society's upper echelon (Trow, 2001). Until recently in our nation's history, other groups, including minorities, the poor and working classes, and a majority of women, were denied access to most postsecondary institutions. However, two important pieces of legislation, the Servicemen's Readjustment Act of 1944 and the Higher Education Act of 1965, drastically altered the role of American higher education and "changed forever who could go to college, and what college was for" (Kuh, 2001, p. 279). Today, colleges and universities provide a wide range of education and training to students of increasingly diverse backgrounds. Members of groups that were once disenfranchised now view a college education as a universal equalizer and the key to upward mobility.

Just as higher education has had to alter its purpose to meet the needs of a larger, more heterogeneous population of students, it has also had to re-evaluate the viability of its role as a socializing agent in the new millennium. Much like a family, religion, or the community in which one is reared, higher education has traditionally assumed, or been tasked with, the role of a social institution and in addition to educating students has been responsible for "the cultivation of citizenship, the preservation of cultural heritage[s], and the formation of individual character and critical habits of mind" (Gumport, 2001, p. 87). Those who see higher education as a socializing agent have traditionally viewed the university experience through a liberal arts lens and believe that not only should students enroll in college to obtain a degree that will position them to secure a prestigious job but that their college years should be filled with exploration and self-development. Under this model, students are exposed to a broad range of academic disciplines and encouraged to acquire knowledge simply for the sake of knowing. In this vein, higher education has traditionally been viewed as a community of learners where both faculty members and students have a vested interest in the educational process.

While many agree that higher education has traditionally been a purveyor of cultural norms and values, critics suggest that those who champion this perspective without considering the academy's need to respond to economic forces and calls for greater accountability may contribute to its ultimate demise (Gumport, 2001). If they are to remain competitive during an era when many students view a college education as a prerequisite for a dream job and not as a stepping stone "toward membership in a cultural elite marked by common bodies of arcane knowledge and cultivated ways of thinking and feeling" (Trow, 2001, p. 110), higher education institutions must design new ways to meet consumer expectations and equip students with skills that will enable them to enter the workforce.

Similarly, broad differences between students and faculty members on the purpose of a college education point to the need for higher education reform. In a recent study, 80% of university freshmen reported that preparation for a professional career was a primary reason for attending college, while only 20% of faculty members agreed (Kuh, 2001). In a separate study, 79% of faculty indicated that developing a meaningful philosophy of life was an integral part of the college experience, while only 42% of students thought it important to do so (Sax, Astin, Arredondo, & Korn, 1996; Sax, Astin, Korn, & Mahoney, 1997). These contrasting perspectives reflect evolving notions about the purpose of higher education, and scholars suggest that unwillingness to change with the times will result in "a loss of centrality, and ultimately a loss of viability" for higher education (Gumport, 2001, p. 87).

Changing Student Demographics

Perhaps one of the most discussed areas of change in higher education is the changing demographics of its student population. Rendón and Hope (1996) asserted that the nation's demographic profile was more ethnically and racially diverse than ever before and, consequently, minority children were entering the educational pipeline in increasing numbers. ACE's *Minorities in Higher Education 2002-2003: Twentieth Annual Status Report* (Harvey, 2003) confirmed that in the past 20 years, minorities have made significant progress in higher education. However, they continue to lag behind their White counterparts in key areas of achievement, high school completion, college participation, and graduation. For example, in 1998, 67% of White high school graduates continued their education at a post-secondary institution. In the same year, the college-going rates of Blacks and Latinos were 61% and 47%, respectively.

Today's college students are different than previous generations in several other ways, too. Traditional-age college students (18-22) who are enrolled full-time and reside on campus with no work experience are rare. In fact, in 1993 less than 20% of all undergraduates fit this profile. Instead, 38% of students were over 25 years old, 42% were enrolled part-time, and 61% were employed to some degree (Levine, 2001). By 1998, the proportion of enrolled students who were at least 25 years old had increased to 45% (Kuh, 2001).

Gender patterns have changed as well. In a review of data from 1966 to 1996, Astin (1998) found that the American college student had changed in ways that were significant. The educational and career aspirations of women expanded, as did the attitude about the role of women in society. Over the years, women have demonstrated an increased interest in pursuing advanced degrees, whereas male interest in fields like law decreased and only increased slightly in other graduate fields. The social, political, and cultural shift in women's aspirations has resulted in women outpacing men in college attendance across all groups (Harvey & Anderson, 2005).

Today's students also come from different familial structures and deal with more emotional distress than those of previous generations. For example, the proportion of children residing in single-parent homes more than doubled from 1960 to 1986 (Hansen, 1999). Additionally, in 1997, the percentage of first-year college students from divorced families (26%) was 3 times higher than in 1972. A survey of college counseling center directors (Gallagher, 1995) found that from 1980 to 1995, the rate of college student suicide attempts increased by 23% and incidence of eating disorders increased by 58%. Thus, Levine and Cureton (1998) suggest that today, more college students are psychologically damaged, require hospitalizations for psychiatric reasons, or have serious problems that are treated by psychoactive medications than at any other point in history.

Finally, scholars contend that many of today's college students have not received adequate secondary school training. Most college professors agree that students are less academically prepared and inclined to read than previous cohorts of students (Trow, 2001). To equip students with the fundamental writing, speaking, and mathematical skills needed for success in college, many institutions offer remedial courses. Hansen (1999) found that 75% of all postsecondary institutions offered remedial coursework, and that approximately 30% of all undergraduates enrolled in one or more such courses.

Access and the Rising Cost of Higher Education

There are many personal and societal benefits of obtaining a college education, and research shows that a college degree is a prerequisite for the career paths that lead to the largest financial rewards. Hurwitz and Hurwitz (2002) asserted that in 1999, the average annual income for college and high school graduates was $48,517 and $26,099, respectively. Mortenson (2000) argued that in nearly every respect, individuals who are college-educated enjoy a higher standard of living, are happier, and have longer life expectancies, better health, and increased productivity when compared with those without a college degree.

The economic benefits are clear. Yet research also suggests that higher education participation rates are closely linked to socioeconomic status; hence, a person's opportunity to enjoy the benefits of obtaining a college degree depends, in part, on income level. In an effort to eliminate the college participation gap between high- and low-income students, Congress passed the Higher Education Act (HEA) of 1965, which sought to "narrow over time the unacceptable income-related gaps existing in postsecondary participation, persistence, and degree completion" (Fitzgerald & Delaney, 2002, p. 6). One of the major tenets of the HEA was the federal student aid program, which provided financial assistance to low-income students whose families could not afford to pay all or part of their tuition and college-related expenses.

The original Higher Education Act, along with the 1972 amendments, made college more affordable. In fact, the federal aid programs were successful in "ensur[ing], at a minimum, that the decision of lower-income students to attend either a two-year or a four-year public institution full time would not be unduly constrained by high unmet need and the consequent necessity to work or to borrow excessively" (Fitzgerald & Delaney, 2002, p. 8).

Additionally, at its height, the Pell Grant program (which served as a cornerstone of the HEA) not only improved access to public institutions but in many cases provided enough funding for low-income students to be able to afford to attend some private institutions. During 1975-1976, the dollar amount of the maximum Pell Grant covered over 80% and 40% of the costs of attending a four-year public or private institution, respectively (Fitzgerald & Delaney, 2002).

As a result of federal and state initiatives, all segments of the nation's population have benefited from increased access to higher education. However, low-income students continue to attend college at lower rates than their high-income counterparts: Attendance gaps are as wide today as they were 30 years ago (Gladieux & Swail, 1998). For example, in 1994, 67% of students from the highest income quartile attended college, while only 20% of those from the lowest quartile did so (Gladieux & Swail, 1998). Additionally, Hurwitz and Hurwitz (2002) found that even the brightest students' decisions to attend college were influenced by their incomes, and that high-achieving students from low-income families were 5 times less likely to attend college than their more economically advantaged peers.

In a 10-year longitudinal study on college access and persistence, Choy (2002) found that over 90% of high school graduates of all income levels planned to continue their education at a postsecondary institution. However, family income and parents' educational attainment greatly influenced whether students executed their plans within two years of graduating. The study revealed that while in 1992, 94% of students with family incomes of less than $25,000 planned to attend college, only 64% had actually enrolled by 1994. Conversely, of students with family incomes of $75,000 or more, 99% aspired to attend college and 93% had actually matriculated in a postsecondary institution within two years.

Scholars suggest that the differences in the college participation rates of students of different income levels can be attributed, in part, to a decreased commitment to postsecondary access by the government. Mortenson (2000) noted that in the early 1980s, states began allocating a declining share of their resources to higher education funding, and in 2000 state tax resources for postsecondary institutions were 77% below their 1979 peak. Similarly, Orfield (1993) asserted that in the late 1970s, federal and state governments that once staunchly supported making higher education available to students from low-income families began to change their positions as a result of political pressures from the middle class. The nation's decreasing commitment to higher education funding for the economically disadvantaged culminated in the 1992 reauthorization of the Higher Education Act, which established new loan programs and broadened eligibility guidelines so that families with more wealth could receive financial assistance. This resulted in a greater dependence on loans as the major source of student financial aid. These changes in higher education funding led to students and families being responsible for paying a greater percentage of college costs and to postsecondary education becoming less affordable and accessible for many students.

Fitzgerald and Delaney (2002) argued that in 1995, the lowest-income students had $3,200, $3,800, and $6,000 of unmet need at community colleges, four-year public, and private institutions, respectively. For low-income families, $4,000, or the average amount of unmet need, was equivalent to one sixth of the annual income of their households. The authors suggested that, "it is quite apparent that excessive unmet need is forcing many lower-income students to choose levels of enrollment and financing alternatives not conducive to academic success, persistence, and ultimately, degree completion at any institution type" (Fitzgerald & Delaney, 2002, p. 16). Such evidence supports the assertion that the cost of college attendance continues to serve as a formidable barrier to postsecondary access for many of the country's poorest students and illustrates the inadequacy of current financial aid policies.

The Impact of Technology

The rapid emergence of new technology has changed every aspect of American culture. The field of education faces both opportunities and challenges in deciding how technology can enhance teaching and access to education and expand research practice. Pascarella and Terenzini (1998) observed that the shifts in technological changes, demographics, and economic forces have revolutionized the conventional understanding of relationships between faculty and students, the teaching and learning process, and the ways in which faculty and students interact inside and outside of the classroom. Essentially, technology has created new understanding of and options for how teaching occurs, what is considered the domain of the classroom, and the roles of the learner and teacher in the use of technology.

Trow (2001) argued that technology presents the most formidable change because it has the potential to transform every other aspect of postsecondary education. Technology will revolutionize higher education in America and abroad by minimizing geographic barriers, reducing the need for physical campuses, redefining the nature of the student-teacher relationship, and altering the role of for-profit institutions (Levine, 2001). The ultimate test is whether traditional colleges and universities can keep pace with the dizzying rate of change imposed by technological advances.

Technologies change at a rapid pace that is counter to the way universities implement change. In order to affect change on a college or university campus, one must typically proceed through a series of committee meetings, administrative reviews, and policy examinations. It can routinely take an entire academic year, or longer, to modify an operating procedure. Conversely, in today's world, technologies are developed so rapidly that it is sometimes difficult to pinpoint exactly when an innovation emerged on the scene. Wilson (2001) argued that these technological advances "change the world in dramatic ways on a time scale so much faster than the usual university responses that the effects, not surprisingly, are disconcerting to everyone" (p. 203).

Higher education scholars and administrators tend to agree that in order to remain current with the times, colleges and universities must implement responses to the widespread changes that have resulted from the technological revolution (Wilson, 2001). They also concur that a college education must equip today's students to thrive in a technologically driven environment, in which new applications will continue to reshape many professions. However, there is little consensus as to how this lofty objective can be best achieved. In order for college graduates to be successful in modern society, Wilson (2001) said that they must be able to use and assess technology as it pertains to their occupations. To this end, postsecondary institutions should create opportunities for students to become comfortable using various technological devices and applications.

Students and Their Learning

Pascarella and Terenzini (1998) submitted that studying students in the 21st century brings new challenges to the field of higher education. They asserted that we know much more about the conditions that foster student learning and development than we used to know. These conditions include "small institutional size, a strong faculty emphasis on teaching and student development, a student body that attends college full-time and resides on campus, a common general education emphasis or shared intellectual experience in the curriculum, and frequent interaction in and outside the classroom between students and faculty and between student and their peers" (Pascarella & Terenzini, pp. 151-152).

In addition to knowing more about the conditions that foster learning, we also have more insight into how students learn and develop (Baxter Magolda, 1992; Baxter Magolda, 2000; Howard-Hamilton, 2000; Howell & Tuitt, 2003; Ignelzi, 2000; King, 2000; Schroeder, 1993; Silverman & Casazza, 2000), which is often counter to how professors teach. We know that many students prefer moderate to high structure and concrete experiences and tend to be linear in their approach to learning, whereas faculty tend to be more stimulated by global issues and broad concepts (Schroeder, 1993). Research indicates that over time, students' ways of learning change and reflect more complex thinking patterns (Baxter Magolda, 1992). Students enter the classrooms with distinct backgrounds and unique experiences that mediate their learning (Baxter Magolda, 2000). Although educators cannot possibly understand each student's journey, it is important to understand how students make meaning out of their experiences and use these experiences to understand what they learn in the classroom. The diverse learning styles and experiences of students create challenges for faculty whose educational experiences and backgrounds tend to reflect traditional paradigms of learning and predictable cultural experiences.

At a time in which we feel we know more about college students and their learning, we also face significant challenges in demographic trends, economic conditions, and societal changes that will alter who is coming to college and the conditions that affect their success (Pascarella & Terenzini; 1998). Pascarella and Terenzini observed that these changes will challenge us to think differently about our research on college students, including how we collect data. The diversity of our student body will necessitate expanding our research traditions to include more than traditional methods.

Pascarella and Terenzini (1998) also called our attention to the important role of community colleges in understanding the needs of a changing student body. Community colleges have always provided education for nearly one third of students entering higher education. They have increasingly become the gateway to education for many students, particularly minority students (Rendon & Hope, 1996). While most of the research on college students focuses on those attending traditional four-year institutions, research on community colleges (Deegan & O'Banion, 1989; O'Banion, 1997; Harvey-Smith, 2003) reveals the important role they play in the development of students. Because community colleges represent some of the best examples in diverse campus environments, we must invest in understanding their effectiveness and impact.

Perhaps some of the most significant work on students and their learning at the community college level has emerged from the work of Terry O'Banion (1997) and the learning college initiative. Motivated by the calls for change in the 1980s and more recently the Wingspread Group's "An American Imperative: Higher Expectations for Higher Education" (1993), O'Banion sought to provide a framework for how to focus on the reforms in higher education that put students and their learning first. He identified a number of steps that colleges need to employ to launch a learning college: build a critical coalition, create an emerging vision, involve all stakeholders, ensure appropriate support, create an open system of communication, consider consultants and established processes, pay attention to language, reallocate resources, evaluate the process of change, and be committed for the long term.

O'Banion advises institutions to "capitalize on a natural trigger event" to launch a learning college. A trigger event "releases energy and creates opportunity, an event that leaders can use to focus thought and to rally troops to action" (1997, p. 227). Using O'Banion's framework, Harvey-Smith (2003) conducted a study of several community colleges seeking to adopt the learning paradigm in student affairs. Her study confirmed O'Banion's work and also found a seventh principle that centers on creating and nurturing an organizational culture that is not only open to change but is responsive to change and the learning process. Harvey-Smith found that the seventh principle is pivotal to the process and provides the basis for the six other principles to develop.

CONCLUSION

Undergirding all of these calls for change are demands for learning organizations to equip students of varied backgrounds for success in what Levine (2001) terms an "information society," where intellectual capital is the most valuable and rewarded commodity, as opposed to physical labor and natural resources, which were considered premium assets during the industrial era. The ability of colleges to become agents of change in the learning and development of students is essential.

Institutions that are committed to cultivating environments in which students can be academically, socially, and psychologically successful have to be willing to investigate and confront the barriers that impede their success. Those who teach students must recognize that students are cocreators in the learning process and understand that they bring a set of values and beliefs into the academy that help to shape the experiences of their peers in and outside of the classroom. Faculty must be encouraged to expand their pedagogic practices and to regularly evaluate how their own beliefs, values, and attitudes shape the environment of the classroom. Faculty who are willing to confront their own intellectual domination in the classroom are likely to be open to new ways of teaching and learning. Student affairs can be vital in cultivating these environments of learning. Administrators and other levels of staff should be challenged to think critically about policies and programs designed to meet the needs of students. The calls for change in postsecondary higher education are extensive and at times overwhelming. Nonetheless, they serve as a source of motivation because they challenge our capacity to be creative, persistent, innovative, and responsive to the needs of the students we serve.

REFERENCES

American Association of Colleges and Universities. (2002). *Greater expectations.* Washington, DC: Author.

American College Personnel Association and National Association of Student Personnel Administrators. (2004). *Learning reconsidered: A campus-wide focus on the student experience.* Washington, DC: American College Personnel Association and National Association.

Astin, A. (1998). The changing American college student: Thirty-year trends, 1966-1996. *The Review of Higher Education, 21*(2), 115-135.

Astin, A. W., & Astin, H. S. (Eds.). (2000). *Leadership reconsidered: Engaging higher education in social change.* Battle Creek, MI: W. K. Kellogg Foundation.

Baxter Magolda, M. B. (1992). *Knowing and reasoning in college: Gender-related patterns in students' intellectual development.* San Francisco: Jossey-Bass.

Baxter Magolda, M. B. (2000). *Teaching to promote intellectual and personal maturity: Incorporating students' worldviews and identities into the learning process. New directions in teaching and learning,* No 82. San Francisco: Jossey-Bass.

Choy, S. P. (2002). *Access & persistence: Findings from 10 years of longitudinal research on students.* Washington, DC: American Council on Education.

College Board. (1999). *Reaching the top: Report of the National Task Force on Minority High Achievement* (Item No. 201635). New York: Author.

Deegan, W. L., & O'Banion, T. (1989). *Perspectives on student development. New directions for community colleges,* No. 67. San Francisco: Jossey-Bass.

Fitzgerald, B. K., & Delaney, J. A. (2002). Educational opportunity in America. In D.E. Heller (Ed.), *Condition of access: Higher education for lower income students* (pp. 3-24). Westport, CT: Prager Publishers.

Gallagher, R. P. (1995). *National survey of counseling center directors, 1995.* Alexandria, VA: International Association of Counseling Services.

Gladieux, L., & Swail, W. (1998). Financial aid is not enough. *The College Board Review, 185,* 17-21.

Gumport, P .J. (2001). Built to serve: The enduring legacy of public higher education. In P. G. Altbach, P. J. Gumport, & J. B. Johnstone (Eds.), *In defense of American higher education* (pp. 85-109). Baltimore: The Johns Hopkins University Press.

Hansen, E. J. (1999). Essential demographics of today's college students. *AAHE Bulletin, 51*(3), 3-5.

Harvey, W. B. (2003). *Minorities in Higher Education 2002-2003: Twentieth Annual Status Report.* Washington, DC: American Council on Education.

Harvey, W. B., & Anderson, E. L. (2005). *Minorities in Higher Education 2003-2004: Twenty-first Annual Status Report.* Washington, DC: American Council on Education.

Harvey-Smith, A. B. (2003). *The adoption of the learning paradigm in student affairs divisions in Vanguard community colleges.* Unpublished doctoral dissertation, University of Maryland, College Park.

Howard-Hamilton, M. *Programming for Multicultural Competencies. New Directions for Student Services,* No. 90. San Francisco: Jossey-Bass.

Howell, A., & Tuitt, F. (2003). *Race and higher education: Rethinking pedagogy in diverse college classrooms,* Reprint Series No. 36. Cambridge, MA: Harvard Educational Review.

Hurwitz, N., & Hurwitz, S. (2002). Getting into college. *American School Board Journal, 190,* 18-25.

Ignelzi, M. (2000). Meaning-making in the learning and teaching process. In M. Baxter Magolda (Ed.), *Teaching to promote intellectual and personal maturity: Incorporating students' worldviews and identities into the learning process. New directions for teaching and learning,* No. 82. (pp. 5-14). San Francisco: Jossey-Bass.

Joint Task Force on Student Learning. (1998). *Powerful partnerships: A shared responsibility for learning.* American Association for Higher Education, American College Personnel Association, and National Association of Student Personnel Administrators.

King, P. M. (2000). Learning to make reflective judgments. In M. Baxter Magolda (Ed.), *Teaching to promote intellectual and personal maturity: Incorporating students' worldviews and identities into the learning process. New directions for teaching and learning,* No. 82 (pp.15-26). San Francisco: Jossey-Bass.

Kuh, G. (2001). College students today: Why we can't leave serendipity to chance. In P. G. Altbach, P. J. Gumport, & J. B. Johnstone (Eds.), *In defense of American higher education* (pp. 277-303). Baltimore: The Johns Hopkins University Press.

Kuh, G. D., Miller, T., Lyons, J., & Trow, J. (1995). *Reasonable expectations: Renewing the educational compact between institutions and students.* Washington, DC: National Association of Student Personnel Administrators.

Levine, A. (2001). Higher education as a mature industry. In P. G. Altbach, P. J. Gumport, & J. B. Johnstone (Eds.), *In defense of American higher education* (pp. 38-58). Baltimore: The Johns Hopkins University Press.

Levine, A., & Cureton, J. S. (1998). Collegiate life: An obituary. *Change, 30*(3), 12-17, 51.

Mortenson, T. (2000). Poverty, race, and the failure of public policy: The crisis of access in higher education. *Academe, 86,* 38-43.

National Association of State Universities and Land-Grant Colleges. (2001). *Returning to our roots: Executive summaries of the reports of the Kellogg Commission on the Future of State and Land Grant Universities.* Washington, DC: Author.

O'Banion, T. (1997). *A learning college for the 21st century.* Phoenix, AZ: Oryx Press.

Orfield, G. (1993, March/April). Federal policy and college opportunity: Refurbishing a rusted dream. *Academe, 25*(2), 11-15.

Pascarella, E. T., & Terenzini, T. P. (1998). Studying students in the 21st century: Meeting new challenges. *Review of Higher Education, 21*(2), 151-156.

Rendon, L. I., & Hope, R. O. (1996). *Educating a new majority: Transforming America's educational system for diversity.* San Francisco: Jossey-Bass.

Sax, L. J., Astin, A. W., Arredondo, M., & Korn, W.S. (1996). *The American college teacher: National norms for the 1995-96 HERI faculty survey.* Los Angeles: University of California, Los Angeles, Higher Education Research Institute.

Sax, L. J., Astin, A. W., Korn, W. S., & Mahoney, K. M. (1997). *The American college freshman.* Los Angeles: University of California, Los Angeles, Higher Education Research Institute.

Schroeder, C. (1993). New students—new learning. *Change, 25*(4), 21-26.

Silverman, S. L., & Casazza, M. (2000). *Learning and development: Making connections to enhancing teaching.* San Francisco: Jossey Bass.

Trow, M. (2001). From mass higher education to universal access: The American advantage. In P. G. Altbach, P. J. Gumport, & J. B. Johnstone (Eds.), *In defense of American higher education* (pp. 110-143). Baltimore: The Johns Hopkins University Press.

Wilson, J. M. (2001). The technological revolution: Reflections on the proper role of technology in higher education. In P. G. Altbach, P. J. Gumport, & J. B. Johnstone (Eds.), *In defense of American higher education* (pp. 202-226). Baltimore: The Johns Hopkins University Press.

Wingspread Group on Higher Education. (1993). *An American imperative: Higher expectations for higher education.* Racine, WI: The Johnson Foundation.

CHAPTER 2

The Learning College Concept and Its Compatibility With Student Affairs

Ted James

"The future is a great land; you can not go around it in a day, measure it with a bound, or bind its harvests into a single sheaf. It is wider than vision and has no end."

—Donald G. Mitchell

INTRODUCTION

We are perhaps now nearing the end-of-the-beginning in the transformation of postsecondary institutions into learning-centered organizations. Much has happened since the early calls for a paradigm shift (Boggs, 1993; Barr & Tagg, 1995; O'Banion, 1997) to explore how the learning college concept can be applied in practice to advance reform in higher education. Much still remains to be done to bring about enduring transformational change (Barr, 1998; Harvey-Smith, 2003b; Tagg, 2003). The significance of this learning revolution for people working in student affairs offices in higher education is profound, not least because placing the learner at the center has traditionally been the avowed focus of student affairs work. Therefore, as the learning college concept becomes a reality, student affairs personnel may reasonably expect that the role they play in their institutions is likely to intensify.

This chapter begins by defining the learning college concept and describes how different observers have formulated this concept out of the distinction between the learning paradigm and the instruction paradigm.

The chapter then explores how the learning college concept is easily assimilated by, and compatible with, the work of student affairs because it aligns with the traditional values and philosophy of student affairs, because reaction to the inadequacies of the instruction paradigm has been a common theme in the evolution of student affairs, and because the changing personnel roles needed to operate a learning college harmonize well with the various skills and expertise of student affairs professionals.

LEARNING COLLEGE CONCEPT

There is an old joke about a drunk who is looking for his car keys under a streetlamp late at night. A passer-by asks the drunk what he is doing and, upon hearing the man's situation, offers to help him find the keys. "Whereabouts did you lose the keys?" asks the passer-by. The drunk points toward some bushes about 50 yards away. "Then why are you looking here, rather than over there?" asks the passer-by in amazement. "Obviously, because there is more light here," replies the drunk.

Toward the end of the 20th century, some analysts of education began to feel the same as this passer-by when they surveyed the landscape of higher education in North America and elsewhere. They felt the academy, especially in its function of creating good learning environments for undergraduates, was in denial. Like the drunk, the academy steadfastly continued in a pursuit that was ineffectual, simply because this pursuit was familiar and well lit. The academy refused to abandon traditional approaches to education and seek new ones drawing upon decades of research evidence that pointed to a better model for organizing learning opportunities for students.

In America, a series of forces concurrently at work fueled the fire of educational reform. There was the failure of several years of effort to address what the National Commission on Excellence in Education in 1983 had called the "rising tide of mediocrity that threatens our future" (p. 5). Leonard (1992), assessing progress to date 10 years later, concluded: "The painful truth is that despite the spotlight on schooling and the stern pro-

nouncements of educators, governors, and presidents, . . . school achievement has remained essentially flat over the past two decades" (p.26).
Leonard recommended that " . . . we can no longer improve the education
of our children by improving school as we know it. The time has come to
recognize that school is not the solution. It is the problem" (p.26). Also, a
second wave of reform—aimed at postsecondary education and provoked
by the publication by the Wingspread Group on Higher Education (1993)
of *An American Imperative: Higher Expectations for Higher Education*—
called for " a seamless system that can produce and support a nation of
learners, providing access to educational services for learners, as they need
them, when they need them and wherever they need them" (p.19).

In addition, the cost of maintaining the existing model of higher
education was becoming burdensome. As McClenney and Mingle (1992)
explained: "The dilemma is that the challenges of meeting the expectations
of society are coming at a time when the costs are on the rise and traditional sources of support—state tax dollars—are shrinking" (p. 1). As the
millennium turned, students faced ever-spiraling tuition and other costs
to bridge this funding gap. In response, they became more deliberate
consumers of education—they shopped around more and demanded
improved service.

Linked to increased consumerism were the arrival of the Internet
and the growth in personal computing. Not only did this permit vastly
increased access to information, but a new generation of students grew up,
often technologically more adept than their teachers. This opened the door
to wider competition in higher education and sparked the entry of many
new private providers, such as the University of Phoenix, exploring new
models of access and delivery. The combination of these forces was dubbed
the "learning revolution" (O'Banion, 1997), and its impact was spreading:

> A conversation with any dean in any college in this coun-
> try will confirm the increasingly demanding nature of the
> current generation of students—who insist on method-
> ologies that meet their needs, who insist on accountabil-

ity from their professors, and who want their money back when they get neither. (p. 38)

The learning revolution focused on the need to put learning—and the needs of learners—ahead of the needs of institutions. Educational reform was to be achieved by concentrating on ways to maximize learning experiences for students. The learner was to be placed at the center of the educational universe. This repositioning, suggested Robert Barr and John Tagg (1995), amounted to nothing less than a complete paradigm shift, and their article called "From teaching to learning—A new paradigm for undergraduate education" quickly became the manifesto of the revolution:

> In its briefest form, the paradigm that has governed our colleges is this: A college is an institution that exists to produce instruction. Subtly but profoundly we are shifting to a new paradigm: A college is an institution that exists to produce learning. This shift changes everything. (p. 13)

Barr and Tagg (1995) outlined how the assumptions, features, and outcomes of working within the instruction paradigm were different from those under the learning paradigm. Whereas the former focuses on delivering courses and transferring knowledge to students, the learning paradigm sees students as the producers of their own learning. Rather than a vessel to be filled, the student is a discoverer who explores. This new constructivist approach led to different criteria for institutional success. The instruction paradigm focuses on inputs, resources, curriculum, and enrollment. The quality of education is synonymous with the credentials of the faculty, the collection in the library, the teaching resources in laboratories, and so on. In contrast, the learning paradigm focuses on the quality and quantity of the learning actually acquired by students. It suggests that the evaluation of teachers should be based not on how well they lecture or how thoroughly they examine but on how effectively they assist students to learn inside and outside the classroom.

Furthermore, the instruction paradigm organizes the delivery of teaching into atomized parts: classes, courses, credits, tests, assignments, and grades, which compartmentalize and standardize the learning experience for the convenience of the institution. The learning paradigm, on the other hand, seeks a more holistic and fluid approach to the learning experience, where the student is a more active participant in determining what is learned and how it is evaluated. Lying at the heart of the differences between the instruction and the learning paradigms are their approaches to learning theory. The former views education as linear, cumulative, competitive, and solitary; talent is seen as rare, and grades are normatively distributed. The latter views education as created, interactive, collaborative, and cooperative. It sees talent as abundant, and grades, if they exist at all, are noncompetitive.

Similarly, the instruction paradigm uses definitions of productivity and accountability that examine the costs of delivering teaching resources, whereas the learning paradigm is more concerned with learning outcomes and what these cost to produce for each student. Not surprisingly, each paradigm ascribes quite different roles to faculty and students. The instruction paradigm elevates the teacher and his or her expertise, while the learning paradigm elevates the student and redefines the teacher as a facilitator of learning whose content expertise is less important than the ability to create rich learning environments.

Obviously, the dichotomy outlined in this paradigmatic framework tends to sharpen distinctions, which in practice are more blurred. Understandably, some faculty took exception to the way writers such as Barr and Tagg characterized their profession, arguing the dichotomy was simplistic, exaggerated, and false (Traverso, 1996). Such criticism emphasized that students were not really customers in the way education is accessed, and that earning a credential is not the same type of activity as consuming a sandwich or purchasing a television (Swenson, 1998).

Nonetheless, the paradigm shift took root and sprouted the fruit of the learning college concept. O'Banion (1997) articulated what a college would look like if it was to embrace the learning paradigm and begin to abandon the instruction one. While his focus was on community colleges and how they could meet challenges, he used the word "college" as a generic term for any postsecondary institution. His goal was to provide a blueprint for change that could bring about lasting results: " . . . the concept of the learning college is an attractive idea in embryo that, if nurtured properly, can address many of the current problems facing higher education. It even has the potential of changing the entire architecture of higher education" (1997, p. xvi). In his seminal work, *A Learning College for the 21ˢᵗ Century*, O'Banion defines the learning college concept:

> the purpose of a "learning college" is to place learning first
> in every policy, program and practice in higher education.
> Not research, not politics, but learning. In this transforma-
> tion, everyone . . . becomes focused on improving
> learning. Not grades, not grants, not publications, but
> learning . . . . The time-bound, place-bound, efficiency-
> bound, and role-bound institution is not sufficient to the
> tasks facing us in the 21ˢᵗ century. (1997, p. 47)

Principles of a Learning College

If one were to create a learning college, what would it look like? How would it function differently from existing colleges? What would be its foundations? In other words, how does a college put the learning paradigm into operation? Several writers have answered these questions by formulating sets of principles for the learning college. While these writers often emphasize different aspects of the learning college concept, their principles reveal commonalities that are relevant to student affairs.

O'Banion's Principles

O'Banion (1997) identifies six guiding principles that underlie the formation of a learning-centered post-secondary institution:

1. The learning college creates substantive change in individual learners.

2. The learning college engages learners as full partners in the learning process, with learners assuming primary responsibility for their own choices.

3. The learning college creates and offers as many options for learning as possible.

4. The learning college assists learners to form and participate in collaborative learning activities.

5. The learning college defines the roles of learning facilitators by the needs of the learners.

6. The learning college succeeds only when improved and expanded learning can be documented for its learners.

O'Banion's list stresses how the learning college concept refocuses the work of the college. He concentrates on the outcomes for learners, which are achieved by the experience of being a college student. Although O'Banion (1997) does not mention student affairs specifically, it is clear his vision of the learning college foresees a critical role for service providers:

> a series of services will be initiated to prepare the learner.... The services will include assessing the learner's abilities, achievements, values, needs, goals, expectations, resources, and environmental/situational limitations. A personal profile will be constructed by the learner in consultation with an expert assessor to illustrate what this learner knows, wants to know, and needs to know. A personal learning plan will be constructed from this personal profile. (p. 49)

Much of the expertise to help bring about this vision already exists in student affairs divisions. Student affairs personnel have long been involved in facilitating student orientations and helping students become engaged in their education.

Krakauer's Criteria

In her dissertation thesis at the University of Toronto, Renate Krakauer (2001) expanded the work of O'Banion and others and developed a set of evaluative criteria. Krakauer extracted the characteristics of an ideal learning college from the literature and developed them into a tool for measuring how far institutions had progressed in becoming learning colleges. She then applied this assessment in a case study of her own institution, the Michener Institute for Applied Health Sciences.

Krakauer's assessment tool contains 100 items, which are categorized to evaluate the following nine types of characteristics of the ideal learning college:

1. The learning process
2. Learning content
3. Learning facilitators
4. Learning specialists
5. Learning outcomes
6. Learners
7. Organization
8. Leadership
9. College culture

Krakauer's work provides a comprehensive framework for college personnel to use to assess their own progress. Since the learning college concept rests on shifting the focus from the institution to the learner, this assessment process can be a catalyst for action as well as provide baseline data for future comparisons. Student affairs divisions have not always assessed their own work, often relying on axiomatic beliefs in the value of their services. Nonetheless, student affairs professionals have commonly been focused on ways to empower students to be active in their own learning. Krakauer's characteristics echo that traditional focus.

Tagg's Characteristics

In their early work on defining and contrasting the instruction and learning paradigms, Barr and Tagg (1995) did not outline a set of characteristics for the learning college per se. However, Tagg (2003) in his later book, *The Learning Paradigm College,* provides "an interpretive framework" for helping college personnel to develop learning-centered institutions. Within that framework, Tagg provides six categories to examine how effective the learning environment is in a college or university:

1. Promotes intrinsically rewarding goals for students
2. Requires frequent, continual, connected, and authentic performances from students
3. Provides consistent, continual, and interactive feedback to students
4. Provides a long time horizon for learning
5. Creates purposeful communities of practice
6. Aligns all activities around the mission of producing student learning

Tagg's set of characteristics is largely similar to O'Banion's six principles in focusing on the outcomes for students that the learning college fosters, but Tagg concentrates on the learning process and what features the institution should facilitate. Like Krakauer's criteria, Tagg's characteristics are evaluative and allow an institution to assess the extent to which it has moved toward becoming an ideal learning-centered institution. Tagg's, however, are less detailed than Krakauer's and are intended as a conceptual framework rather than a measurement tool.

EVOLUTION OF STUDENT AFFAIRS

Student affairs as a construct is relatively new in higher education. Rhatigan (2000) in his overview of the history of student affairs points out that although some writers have suggested student affairs has antecedents in Athenian education and the European universities of the Middle Ages, the field "is largely an American higher education invention. It had a small but important beginning in the nineteenth century, but for the most part is a twentieth century phenomenon" (p. 5).

Student affairs is compatible with the learning college concept because both are somewhat at odds with the instruction paradigm and its narrow perspective on the needs of students within the academy. The role of student affairs has evolved, but it always has moved toward a learner-based perspective. This evolution can be loosely divided into the phases of paternalism, personnelism, developmentalism, and partnerism.

Paternalism

Inherited from the strong moral orientation of higher education previously, the role of the first administrators of student affairs was singular but vague. As deans of male and female students, they were charged with inculcating values in the abstract but were increasingly drawn into the murky practicalities of overseeing student discipline and housing. From around the turn of the century to the mid-1920s, these deans served essentially in loco parentis to oversee the needs of the student body.

Personnelism

From the mid-1920s to the late 1960s, a number of developments led to viewing students as "personnel" to be advised, trained, and managed to take their appropriate place as newly minted employees in the industrialized world. These developments ranged from the influence of John Dewey's views on experiential education to Walter Dill Scott's application of psychological principles to industry, and included Alfred Binet's tests and John B. Watson's behavioral psychology. These forces helped push the profession into a more institutionalized and compartmentalized role.

Developmentalism

Toward the end of the 1960s, the profession of student affairs came increasingly under the influence of various "student development" theories.

The dramatic social and political upheavals that campuses had witnessed during the 1960s, including race riots, Vietnam War protests, and the Sexual Revolution, ushered in a desire to base the profession on more than simply providing personnel services. Instead, as writers Brown (1972) and Crookston (1973) argued, the profession was to enhance the social and intellectual development of students. Students were viewed as being on a continuum of development, and campuses were seen, in effect, as laboratories of life where the development of students could be fostered. To underscore the change, many campuses created or renamed departments of student development.

Partnerism

Beginning with the release of *A Nation at Risk* by the National Commission on Excellence in Education (1983), and continuing with other calls for educational reform in the 1990s, a "learning revolution" began to spread like a forest fire through the landscape of higher education as the millennium turned.

This movement gained fuel from the relentless invasion of computer-based educational technology, which uncoupled the creation and reception of curriculum, freeing students from a time-bound, place-bound delivery of education as the Internet opened new avenues of access to information for students. The movement was also influenced by cries for greater accountability measures and outcome assessment from legislators and others.

As the "learning revolution" called for learning-centered approaches, institutions explored new ways of treating students as customers and consumers of education rather than as simply "students" on campus. Administrators slowly began to view students as partners in the academic enterprise, and students began to demand improved services and more say in their education.

Student affairs professionals were in the thick of this revolution, as adopters of new technology and pioneers in the design and delivery of learning-centered services. They easily embraced the new relationship with students as partners—in contrast to many instructional faculty members who felt threatened and bemused by the shift in organizational power and the loss of autonomy.

VALUES AND PRINCIPLES OF STUDENT AFFAIRS

Another way that the concept of the learning college is a natural fit with student affairs lies in the traditional values and principles espoused by student affairs professionals (Harvey-Smith, 2003a). We've seen how the role of the professional evolved yet retained a focus on treating the student as a whole person. Throughout its evolution, this core was reformulated but always was emphasized by each new generation of student affairs personnel. Let's examine in more detail what constitutes this core.

An early articulation of the common beliefs that underlie the philosophy of student affairs was expressed by Walter Dill Scott in 1919 as the new president of Northwestern University. He described student affairs as a program designed to address individuality. This emphasis resonates in compatibility with the focus of the learning college:

> It is my belief that the emphasis would be on the individuality of the student and his present needs and interests. The student should be looked upon as more than a candidate for a degree, he is an individuality that must be developed and must be trained for a life of service . . . . (quoted in Rhatigan, 2000, p. 11)

The emphasis on individuality was often expanded and embellished by student affairs professionals down through the years. Yet the core of the philosophy endured and deepened. For instance, during the height of the Personnelism phase, Lloyd-Jones and Smith (1954) outlined four common beliefs of student personnel workers (see Figure 1). The first belief echoed Scott's emphasis on individuality. The second reinforced the holistic aspect of student affairs work. The third belief extends the concept forward into helping students fulfill their potential. The final belief reinforces the value of what is learned rather than what is taught, and it foreshadows the later interest by the profession in students in transition. Again, these beliefs correspond well to the tenets of the learning college concept with its focus on the individual experience of learners and emphasis on the importance of concentrating on the learner's needs rather than those of the institution.

Figure 1: Common Beliefs of Student Personnel Workers
(Lloyd-Jones and Smith, 1954)

1. *A belief in the worth of the individual*; that human values are of greatest importance; that the common good can be promoted best by helping each individual to develop to the utmost in accordance with his abilities....

2. *The belief in the equal dignity of thinking and feeling and working*; that these aspects are inseparable. Personnel work is interested in the *whole* person and not merely in his mind or his economic productivity or some other one of his aspects.

3. *The belief that the world has a place for everyone*: a place in the social world, a place in the civic world, a place in family life, and a place in the vocational world; that it is education's task to offer youth not only an invitation, but also positive stimulation carefully adapted to his needs to help him grow to full stature in all of these roles....

4. *The belief that what an individual gathers from his experiences continues on in time*; it is not what is imposed, but what is absorbed that persists. Personnel workers see the person – at whatever age – not as a single moment independent of the past and future, but as a transition point in a stream of experience....

[Note: emphasis added]

This emphasis on learners' needs is also reflected in more contemporary expressions of the philosophy of student affairs. In the past decade, as the learning revolution has gained momentum, student affairs associations have begun to reflect the language of the learning revolution more often in their documents.

For example, the Canadian Association of College and University Student Services (CACUSS) produced in 1999 a statement of its guiding principles (see Figure 2). There is the traditional focus on respect for student individuality and growth. There are also assertions of the important role played by student affairs professionals as educators and partners in the institution. But the role of the institution itself—its mission—now gets more prominence along with comments about "quality" and "context" for learning.

Figure 2: Guiding Principles for Student Services
(CACUSS, 1999)

- The mission of the educational institution is paramount.
- Quality of life in a teaching and learning community is crucial to the educational mission.
- Each individual has worth and dignity, and should be treated with respect.
- Post-secondary education should be aimed at an individual's total growth.
- Learning is contextual and is influenced by a wide range of individual and environmental factors.
- Student services professionals are educators.
- The educational goals of post-secondary institutions are best realized through a partnership of student services personnel with students, staff, administrators, and faculty.

Similarly, the ACPA and the NASPA in the United States had adopted, a year earlier, seven principles for good practice in student affairs (see

Figure 3). The traditional expressions of learner-orientation underlie the language employed to express these principles—emphasizing the agency of engaging, helping, and forging, for example. But the language also includes new expressions—such as active learning, high expectations, systematic inquiry, and inclusive communities—that show the effect of the learning revolution and the goals of the learning college.

Figure 3: Principles of Good Practice in Student Affairs
(ACPA/NASPA, 1998)

Good practice in student affairs:

1. Engages students in active learning
2. Helps students build coherent values and ethical standards
3. Sets and communicates high expectations for student learning
4. Uses systematic inquiry to improve student and institutional performance
5. Uses resources effectively to help achieve institutional missions and goals
6. Forges educational partnerships that advance student learning
7. Builds supportive and inclusive communities

NEW ROLES FOR EDUCATORS

The learning revolution calls into question the traditional role played by college employees. Conventionally, faculty members have acted as the providers of information that they package and present to students. In the learning college concept, their role shifts to that of facilitators of student learning, with students having a more active role in what they do and what they learn. Similarly, service staff have acted as gatekeepers of services, where students wait in lines and access services at the institution's convenience. The learning revolution also is changing the way in which services are delivered (see Figure 4). In the process, the role of service staff is shifting from gatekeepers to facilitators, where staff assists students to locate information for themselves and provides a range of support services available in different formats and at different times (Kvavik & Handberg, 2000).

Figure 4: Evolving Student Services
(adapted from Kvavik & Handberg, 2000)

Traditional Way	Future Way
• Students wait in lines	• Learners access services from any computer hooked to the Internet
• Students walk all over campus	• Learners access everything from one location
• Services open 8 hours per day, 5 days per week (perhaps)	• Services available 24 hours per day every day of the year
• Students gather stacks of printed material	• Learners download only what they want and print what they actually need
• College maintains multiple sources of information	• College maintains single electronic site, easily accessed and used
• Provider-focused	• Customer-focused
• Departmental silos	• Seamless service

O'Banion (1997) lists the types of roles for staff and faculty which the learning college concept will promote (see Diagram E). The list provides clear assurance that the skills, talents, and duties of those working in student affairs will not only remain in higher education institutions but also will flourish and prosper.

Figure 5: Roles for Staff and Faculty
(O'Banion, 1997)

• Encourage and facilitate enrollment	• Arrange work-based learning
• Assess student needs	• Arrange service learning
• Encourage attendance and participation	• Nurture interpersonal relationships
• Design learning experiences	• Create connection activities
• Locate resources	• Guide, tutor, coach
• Provide content expertise	• Create standards and outcome measures
• Develop feedback mechanisms	• Conduct research
• Lecture	• Maintain attractive environment
• Lead discussions	• Coordinate systems
• Coordinate field trips	• Provide vision
	• Award credentials

Indeed, the continuing influence of the learning revolution is likely to alter the role played by educational institutions and to draw more heavily on the talents of student affairs professionals. As the demands of students widen, as access to information increases, and as competition to serve students deepens, institutions will search more critically to carve out their niche in the higher education market. Some suggest the pressure will force institutions to differentiate or die (Drucker, 1992; Noam, 1995; Rowley, Lujan, & Dolence, 1998). In response, higher education institutions may turn to student affairs expertise as a competitive advantage (James, 2002). For example, speaking to an audience of community college personnel, Doucette (1998) explained:

> Community colleges should acknowledge what they do
> well, perhaps better than most other institutions. These

colleges have a longstanding commitment to and know-how to support learners . . . . Rather than competing with Microsoft and Disney, community colleges will prosper if they do what they do best: provide learning support services to help students learn, regardless of where they get their information . . . . They should draw upon years of experience in student development, student support services and developmental education to become the best learning support organizations in the world. Disney and Microsoft cannot compete in the provision of these services in support of student learning. In their local communities, this appears a winning strategic market niche for community colleges.

The future for most institutions that embrace the learning college concept is likely to involve a reassessment of the significance of student services as a catalyst propelling these colleges towards a more learning-centered environment. Indeed, the central role of institutions may well become to position themselves to support learning in ways that rely upon the talents of student services professionals:

learning colleges should become providers of learning support services and learning expertise. Their principal function will be to inventory learning options and experiences and to guide and support students accessing them, whether as brokers or deliverers of programming. In so doing, colleges will evolve into formal learning support centers . . . . This vision will have key implications for changing faculty and staff roles—such as the changing role of librarians assisting learners to make sense of information available on the Internet – but it will also move many student support services into mainstream importance in the educational institution. (James, 1999, pp. 73-74)

CONCLUSION

In this chapter we have explored what the learning college concept is and how it is easily embraced by student affairs professionals because it emphasizes common values, student needs, and familiar skills sets. Indeed, this strong compatibility between the two will likely elevate the significance of student affairs in institutions that adopt the learning college concept.

However, as Harvey-Smith (2003a) has already demonstrated, the impact of these changes on student affairs can present new challenges. As student affairs divisions move to espouse the principles of the learning college, the practices and processes of student affairs will be challenged to become more intentional, integrated, and inclusive. Furthermore, student affairs will need to examine more closely how its operations do in fact promote student learning, rather than merely provide services to students. As learning colleges strive to help students "make passionate connections to learning" (O'Banion, 1997, p. xvi), student affairs professionals must affirm their commitment to an educational philosophy of service delivery and must create programming that enhances student learning.

REFERENCES

American College Personnel Association and National Association of Student Personnel Administrators. (1998). *Principles of good practice for student affairs.* Washington, DC: ACPA/NASPA.

Barr, R. B., & Tagg, J. (1995). From teaching to learning: A new paradigm for undergraduate education. *Change, 42*(7), 13-25.

Barr, M. J., Desler, M. K., Ambler, D.A., Bimling, G. S., Carter, K. A., Claar, J., et al. (2000). *The handbook of student affairs administration* (2nd ed.) Publication of the National Association of Student Personnel Administrators. San Francisco: Jossey-Bass.

Barr, R. B. (1998). Obstacles to implementing the learning paradigm: What it takes to overcome them. *About Campus, 2*(3), 18-25.

Boggs, G. (1993, September). Community Colleges and the New Paradigm. *Celebrations.* Austin, TX: National Institute for Staff and Organizational Development.

Brown, R .D. (1972). *Student development in tomorrow's higher education: A return to the academy.* Washington, DC: American College Personnel Association.

Canadian Association of Colleges & University Student Services Conferences (1999).

Crookston, B. (1973). Education for human development. In C. Warnath et al., *New directions for college counselors: A handbook for redesigning professional roles.* San Francisco: Jossey-Bass.

Doucette, D. (1998, May). *Business not as usual in our colleges and universities.* Presentation at Connections '98: Bridging the gap conference, Vancouver, BC, Canada.

Drucker, P. F. (1992). *Managing for the future: The 1990s and beyond.* New York: Dutton.

Harvey-Smith, A. B. (2003a). *The adoption of the learning paradigm in student affairs divisions in Vanguard community colleges.* Unpublished doctoral dissertation, University of Maryland, College Park.

Harvey-Smith, A. B. (2003b) A framework for transforming learning organizations: Proposing a new learning college principle [Electronic version]. *Learning Abstracts, 6*(5).

James, T. (1999). *Learner support and success: Determining the educational support needs for learners into the 21st. century.* Report prepared for the British Columbia Senior Educational Officers Committee and Senior Instructional Officers Committee. http://www.bccat.bc.ca/pubs/learner.pdf

James, T. (2002, June). No longer Cinderella: The future of student development services. Presentation given at the annual conference of the American Association of Community Colleges. Seattle, WA. .

Krakauer, R. (2001). *A learning college for health care: The applicability of learning-centered education to the Michener Institute for Applied Health Sciences.* Unpublished doctoral dissertation, University of Toronto.

Kvavik, R. B., & Handberg, M. N. (2000). Transforming student services. *EDUCAUSE Quarterly, 23*(2), 30-37.

Leonard, G. (1992, May). The end of school. *The Atlantic, 269*(5).

Lloyd-Jones, E., & Smith, M. R. (1954). *Student personnel work as deeper teaching.* New York: Harper and Bras.

McClenney, K., & Mingle, J. Higher education finance in the 1990s: Hard choices for community colleges. *Leadership Abstracts, 5*(7).

National Commission on Excellence in Higher Education. (1983). *A Nation at Risk: The Imperative for Educational Reform.* Washington, DC: Author.

Noam, E. M. (1995, October 13). Electronics and the dim future of the university. *Science.*

O'Banion, T. (1997). *A learning college for the 21st century.* Phoenix, AZ: Oryx Press.

Rowley, D. J., Lujan, H. D., and Dolence, M. G. (1998). *Strategic choices for the academy: How demand for lifelong learning will re-create higher education.* San Francisco: Jossey-Bass.

Swenson, C. (1998). Customers and markets: The cuss words of academe. *Change, 30*(5).

Tagg, J. (2003). *The learning paradigm college.* Bolton, MA: Anker Publishing.

Traverso, E. (1996, December). 'Learning': Buzz word or new insight. *FACCCTS, The Journal of the Faculty Association of the California Community College, 3*(2), 19.

Wingspread Group on Higher Education. (1993). *An American imperative: Higher expectations for higher education.* Racine, WI: Johnson Foundation.

CHAPTER 3

The Seventh Learning College Principle and Organizational Transformation

Alicia B. Harvey-Smith

"There is nothing more difficult to plan, more doubtful of success, nor more dangerous to manage than the creation of a new order of things."

—Niccolo' Machiavelli, The Prince

INTRODUCTION

A*Learning College for the 21st Century* (O'Banion, 1997) established the framework for change for the learning revolution in higher education. Terry O'Banion's six principles refocus the work of the college, putting an emphasis on the outcomes for learners. As a result of my research on organizational change and transformation, I have created a seventh learning college principle that O'Banion and other leaders have endorsed. That principle provides the framework for this book.

The seventh learning college principle is to create and nurture an organizational culture that is both open and responsive to change and learning. This principle has been described as the umbrella principle from which the original principles may emerge (T. O'Banion, personal communication, July 28, 2003). This chapter discusses the seventh learning college principle and shares strategies for actualizing the principle in student affairs divisions and the larger college community.

SUPPORT FOR THE LEARNING COLLEGE PRINCIPLES

In order to create substantive change in learners, an environment must support learning for all students. Systems must connect students to learning experiences in environments that meet their needs, even if those environments are external to our institutions. It is paramount that learning environments embrace the notion that all learners are capable of some measure of success. There must be a willingness to understand and apply new levels of knowledge as it relates to teaching and interacting with diverse members of the community. Innovation and creativity must be applied to learning and then using new teaching modalities and approaches to out-of-class engagement. Institutional cultures must be more responsive and caring.

To effectively engage learners as full partners in the learning process, so they assume primary responsibility for their choices, requires a culture that celebrates the potential of all learners and values students above the systems that serve them. To achieve that goal, cultures must subscribe to the philosophy that all students come into postsecondary education not as blank slates but with some knowledge and wisdom that expand through the learning process.

Redefining institutional roles to meet diverse learners' needs requires an institutional culture that is open to ideas of change and learning. National demographic studies indicate a looming major shift in the number and type of students who will be attending colleges and universities. To respond to the needs of these students, institutional cultures will need to change. Changing does not mean lowering standards but may mean a need for new strategies and expectations. The institutional culture needs to be open to new ways of learning, where diverse learners are valued, innovative strategies are developed to support unique learning styles, and appropriate support systems and safety nets are provided.

STEPS TO ACTUALIZATION

Assessment of Culture

A cultural assessment can help an institution determine what elements in its culture support or deter learning-centeredness. The assessment will provide a snapshot of what community members believe best describes the culture as well as where problems exist. The assessment should be comprehensive and engage all stakeholders. It should gauge the level of information sharing, awareness of and responsiveness to diversity, perceived treatment of community members, the basis on which people are hired or promoted, and leadership defensiveness and willingness to hear divergent views.

Open and Diverse Systems

A system that is flexible and allows a free exchange of information is paramount to the realization of the seventh learning college principle. The system must be comprehensive and responsive to the community of learners and provide support for community members in mediums and approaches they understand. The system should incorporate the diverse perspectives of community members into planning.

Authentic Communication and Input

Using honest, effective communication will aid organizations in implementing this principle, since it requires that a variety of forms and venues connect with learners where they are. The input requested and feedback received should be used to shape the direction of change. Learning environments flourish when members can freely share information and have their ideas influence the outcomes.

Foster Relationships and Human Connections

Institutional transformation will not occur as a result of top-down mandates or from a series of mechanical tasks but will evolve from the appreciation and cultivation of human interactions and relationships.

Organizations that create and nurture environments where there are opportunities to grow and where relationships are fostered and forged greatly enhance their ability to realize the seventh learning college principle.

Risk Taking and Innovation Rewarded

Environments that are responsive and open to change and learning provide safe zones for expression, creativity, and innovation. These cultures support risk taking by community members and celebrate their contributions. Therefore, members do not fear failing.

Cultural Awareness and Sensitivity

Members of the community must be made to feel connected and valued. Diversity is viewed as an important strength. Faculty, staff, and administrators discuss issues of difference and use this new knowledge to serve all learners more effectively. The benefit of this knowledge is seen in the classroom as instructors include diverse representations in the curriculum and do not marginalize learners. The student affairs staff incorporates this information into planning and implementation of support systems that reinforce learning.

All Learning Experiences Valued

Many institutions see the classroom experience as the most vital source for student learning, often to the exclusion of other equally valid learning experiences. However, studies of what students themselves see as their most influential experiences ranked classroom interaction, instructors, and ideas presented by instructors far behind the influence of out-of-class study, peer interactions, involvement with support services, college activities, and independent study activities. The seventh learning college principle seeks to create and nurture environments where the total learning experience is validated and assessed.

Compassion, Appreciation, Respect and Empowerment (CARE) Strategies

Innovation and productivity are accelerated in environments where CARE strategies are used. Cultures where members honestly share opinions on how they are experiencing the environment encourage these elements of growth. The seventh learning college principle aims to establish cultures where CARE techniques are readily incorporated and where community members are appreciated, respected, and empowered to integrate the six core learning college principles.

Assessment Culture

Organizational change and cultural transformation must be evaluated qualitatively and quantitatively through systems that measure effectiveness in achieving outcomes. The assessment process should include personal assessments and reflection surveys to determine shifts in culture and morale.

REDEFINING A CULTURE

Higher education faces the critical challenge of creating and maintaining college environments that attract and sustain the community of learners. To address this challenge, institutions should conduct an analysis to fully understand their culture and should establish ongoing communication on transformation strategies. Then, after assessing supports of and barriers to learning in programs, instruction, services, policies, language, relationships, structures and systems, colleges will move toward greater change.

According to Schein (1990), an organization's culture reveals itself on three levels. The first is the institution's physical artifacts. The second is intangible: policies, rituals, networks, and relationships. It includes such things as celebrations and rewards. The third level is the underlying values and operating principles. This can be exemplified through the espoused and actual behaviors of leaders. In an authentic learning organization, leaders must walk the talk.

An organization's culture acts in somewhat the same way as peer pressure, exerting force on community members to act in a specific fashion. These norms of behavior are common for group members and are continuous because they are handed down almost subconsciously to new members. Only after organizations replace norms of behaviors that hinder institutional progress with ones that have been proven to have some significant benefit will lasting cultural changes occur. Contrary to the views held by Kotter (1996), attending to cultural matters through assessments is critical in the early phases of change and likely will set the stage for the institutionalization of transformation as community members have the opportunity to understand and value the change vision.

Reculturing is the label assigned to this process by Fullan (2001). The reculturing of organizations changes the way things are done. Fullan refers to this process as the *sine qua non* (Latin for something essential) of progress. Like the seventh learning college principle, reculturing emphasizes a collaborative culture that respects differences, seeks to expand relationships, and measures results. The seventh learning college principle encourages learning organizations to serve as a catalyst for transformational change through the creation and nurturing of environments where innovation and risk taking flourish, people and ideas are valued, and systems are flexible and responsive to continuous learning and change.

The Emergence of a Culture of CARE

The seventh learning college principle can be utilized to establish organizational cultures that value community members. The principle encourages the success of the total community, through congruency in practices, policies, institutional systems, and resources diffused through a system that improves and expands learning, while fostering strong relationships based on compassion, appreciation, respect, and empowerment.

Moeller, Snider, and Owen (1999) identified the emergence of a new college culture as one of three themes evident in successful organizations that implemented major change. The seventh learning college principle offers one possible approach as significant change efforts are launched. Key to this model is the importance of leadership and learning. In this model, institutions encourage leadership from all levels of the organization and expect leaders to model espoused behaviors. There should be a focus on learning throughout the organization and a clear commitment to move leadership much deeper into the institution, valuing all students, faculty, and staff as learning leaders.

At institutions seeking to carry out the seventh principle, open and responsive systems strategically involve constituencies, providing opportunities to develop and implement innovative strategies in a risk-friendly environment. These emerging cultures are places where learning transformation is the goal and the college community can substantively discuss learning-centered principles.

When institutions embrace a philosophy focused on creating and nurturing environments, the culture becomes more open to the creativity and innovation in its systems. As systems and people are nurtured, new networks and relationships are sustained. All learners are better off.

Architecturally, these environments solicit stakeholder involvement and flatten the hierarchy and college bureaucracy, incorporating multidirectional communication, collaborative processes, shared governance, and innovative decision-making structures. The evolving organizational structure allows greater openness to new ideas and supportive learning experiences. Learning-centered cultures establish feedback mechanisms so the community of learners can initiate and respond to proposed changes. The need for change should be communicated with invitations to talk and learn about challenges at the institution. Organizations that incorporate the seventh learning college principle generate cultures that value communication and possess a sense of obligation to the community of learners, allowing input early in the process.

Key to actualizing the seventh principle will be overcoming historical barriers such as institutional inertia, traditional architecture, fear of change, apathy, cynicism, defensiveness, long-standing rules and practices, and the lack of recognition. Not responding to these challenges can derail potential transformations.

The emerging cultures implementing the seventh learning college principle will be imbued with a commitment to assessment, as a result of nurturing a culture that is responsive to changing the way learning is documented. Building a culture of evidence that transcripts out-of-class learning, involvement in clubs and organizations, leadership experiences, orientation and engagement with support services, and where there is an abandonment of excuses as to why an approach could not be tried will expand the institution's view of learning and leadership.

Supportive cultures celebrate differences through practices supporting the evolution of its members as a collective. These concepts lead to collaborative processes that aid in the transformation of the culture by building trust and opening communication channels. Innovative practices are communicated through a variety of mediums to arrive at mutual understanding. New languages emerge that focus on learning outcomes and encourage students to synthesize their learning and take greater responsibility for their development. These new languages and expectations are integrated into all institutional communications, policies, and practices.

Key to realizing the seventh learning college principle will be the ability to assess institutional change potential and readiness for change. How can the culture be readied for change? Change is contingent on the people implementing it. Conner and Clawson (2004) opined that people are typically pragmatic and thus willing to learn what is needed in order to do their jobs more effectively. It should be recognized that everyone is a learner, and each learner learns differently and at a different rate. Therefore, as learning options are provided for students, the same approach should be applied to the learning of faculty and staff members and administrators as changes are introduced. Learning options can be provided in forms and at rates that will ready cultures for change and enable all learners to understand, connect, and become a part of the change.

Often, institutional change is approached in a hurried, unplanned fashion and is viewed by many community members as too much, too soon. When this occurs, the people who must implement changes feel ignored. The mentality of moving with or without all passengers on board can be disastrous: This strategy presents the illusion of leadership and transformation without true change taking hold. People want to feel included in the process of decision making. Allowing those in the community to see their role in change and where they fit in enables transformation to take shape, creates champions for change, and builds critical mass. One of the most significant components of creating and nurturing cultures that are open and responsive to change and learning is acknowledging past successes.

As change is initiated, people will look to each other for reassurance. Effective leaders during this period will find ways to demonstrate value and respect for these relationships while fostering new networks and connections. As new cultures are constructed, finding ways to help community members build confidence and belief in the organization will improve overall effectiveness.

CONCLUSION

The first step to actualizing the seventh learning college principle is to conduct an audit to gain understanding of the current status of the culture. Next, institutional leaders should model espoused behaviors. Also core to the actualization process are authentic communication and collaboration practices. Moreover, community members who have counter views should be incorporated into the change process and made to feel they have a stake in the outcomes.

Environments focused on creating cultures that are open and responsive to change and learning will need to communicate the benefits of change in a manner that is understandable. Community members wishing to actualize the seventh principle are willing to enhance awareness of diverse cultures in the organization and work to remove barriers that hinder change and learning. Valuing the past, planning the future collectively, and honoring relationships will help institutions create and nurture cultures that are responsive to change and learning.

Figure 1 summarizes key strategies necessary for actualizing the seventh learning college principle.

Figure 1: Actualizing The Seventh Principle

Harvey-Smith, 2003 ©

The Seventh Learning College Principle:	Strategies for Actualizing the Seventh College Principle
Create and nurture an organizational culture that is open and responsive to change and learning.	• Ready cultures for change and transformation by first assessing current culture through an audit or assessment. • Leaders must model espoused behaviors. • Authentic communication is used to gather input and share information. • Risk taking and innovation are encouraged and rewarded. • All community members are seen as learners, and learning is woven into all plans for change. • Stakeholders are provided ongoing opportunities for input and can see how input has shaped the change direction. • The benefits of change are communicated in a manner that stakeholders understand. • Past contributions are acknowledged and reflected upon. • Relationships, connections, and networks are fostered, and new ones are forged. • The college supports the elements represented by cultures of CARE–compassion, appreciation, respect, and empowerment. • The college's vision, mission, and philosophy are aligned in support of learning and cultural transformation where all learners and learning are validated. • Feedback is regularly sought and used to adopt and adapt the change direction. • Blended partnerships and collaborations are utilized to develop conceptual models in service to the community of learners. • The complexity of the individual is respected. • Performance reviews focus on what has been learned and how the position has reinforced learning and transformation. • Organizational leaders explore underlying values, assumptions, beliefs, and expectations of themselves and the community of learners.

A cultural change of this type will lead to systems that are more open and responsive to change and learning. Differences are appreciated as the result of higher levels of trust, collaboration, and inclusion. Levels of communication are deeper, and more attention is paid to building community. Institutions that devote greater attention to creating and nurturing organizational cultures that are open and responsive to change and learning may provide a pivotal foundation that can be transformational for students and all those charged with improving and expanding their learning.

REFERENCES

Conner, M. L., & Clawson, J. G. (2002). *Creating a learning culture.* The Darden School Foundation: Charlottesville, VA.

Fullan, M. (2001). *Leading in a culture of change.* San Francisco: Jossey-Bass.

Harvey-Smith, A. B. (2003). *The adoption of the learning paradigm in student affairs divisions in Vanguard community colleges.* Unpublished doctoral dissertation, University of Maryland, College Park.

Kotter, J. P. (1996). *Leading change.* Boston: Harvard Business School Press.

Moeller, M., Snider, R. M., & Owen, P. (1999). *Can a college structure enhance learning?* Speech at International Conference of the Chair Academy Long Beach, CA. (ERIC Document Reproduction Service No. ED 434 701).

O'Banion, T. (1997). *A learning college for the 21st century.* Phoenix, AZ: Oryx Press.

Schein, E. H. (1990). *Organizational culture in leadership.* San Francisco: Jossey-Bass.

CHAPTER 4

Educational Change Models

Vincent Mumford

"We must change in order to survive."

—Pearl Bailey

INTRODUCTION

While many in the academy are calling for educational change and reform, most of those calling for change do not understand the intricacies of change itself. Understanding the process of change will help institutions better communicate, plan, implement, measure, and evaluate change. Institutions of higher education must not only understand the change process, they must learn to develop systemic change plans that are guided by theory, research, and best practices. They must thoroughly understand the forces that drive change, how their employees will react to change, and the underlying principles of change. But just what is change, and how does it take place within the educational setting?

Defining change is the easy part. Simply speaking, change means "to alter, to make different; to transform, or to cause to pass from one state to another" (Merriam-Webster, 2004). A much harder task is determining how change takes place, since it happens in many ways.

PROVIDING MOMENTUM FOR CHANGE

That's true, in part, because effective institutional change processes are cyclical and continuous, with no clear beginning or end. The Energy Transformation Cycle is an effective tool for helping stakeholders both understand how change takes place and make change happen. It was adapted from the work of W. Edwards Deming (Walton, 1986).

Figure 1: The Energy Transformation Cycle

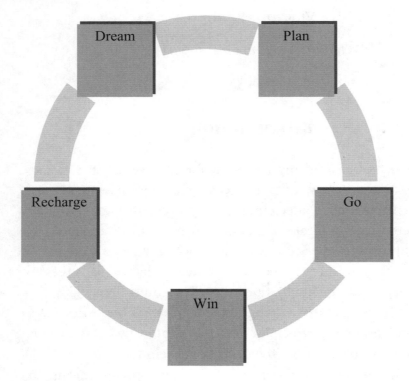

The five processes of the Energy Transformation Cycle can provide momentum for change:

1. **Share the dream:** If your goal is to strengthen student learning and development, share it with as many people as possible. Ask faculty and staff to engage in the dreaming process. Solicit their suggestions. Engage them in brainstorming. Sharing your dream with others helps paint the big picture and gives them something to buy into. It also helps communicate what things are important in your organization. Dreaming helps you decide what is important.

2. **Develop a game plan:** People like to know where they are going. Show them where they are headed by outlining a vision and

strategy for change. A clear vision and action plan give employees direction and confidence. A game plan also helps ensure that all employees are focused on the same results. Involve your faculty and staff in the planning process. Give them a framework and let them develop strategic objectives and goals. They are more likely to stay motivated if they see exactly how their individual goals relate to the goals of the institution and the system. Planning helps you prioritize what is important.

3. **Get up and go:** Once you have fully developed the game plan, do something with it. Find a way to focus the energy and resources of every faculty and staff member on the things that are most important to the success of your institution. Give employees challenging work or committee assignments related to implementing change. Action creates a feeling of energy. Energy creates a feeling of excitement. Taking action helps you do what is important.

4. **Keep score to win:** Keeping score helps you learn and improve. To be successful, you must translate the vision of your institution or system into a set of key performance indicators that can be measured. Those key indicators must assess the institution's progress toward achieving goals and objectives. Use the employee appraisal process as a tool, for example. Let employees conduct self-appraisals evaluated against departmental or institutional expectations. The change agent—the person implementing change—must keep everyone aware of the score at all times. Keeping score helps your institution monitor its current performance, improve processes, motivate and educate employees, and enhance communication. Keeping score helps you measure what is important.

5. **Celebrate to recharge:** Your faculty and staff need to be rewarded for achieving goals and passing milestones. Celebrating their accomplishments underscores the value that each person brings to the table and confirms that expectations concerning behavior have been met. Celebrating also motivates people to learn. Celebrations can be as simple as a pat on the back or a congratulatory e-mail or as complex as a full-blown pep rally. Regular recognition keeps the work exciting. Celebrating helps reward what is important.

DIFFERENT APPROACHES TO MAKING CHANGE HAPPEN

Change agents do not need to reinvent the wheel to make change happen at their institution. They do need to focus on communication and keeping the morale and productivity of faculty and staff high. This can be accomplished by fundamentally rethinking work relationships and aligning work systems.

Several prominent educational change models describe different approaches to achieving change. An educational change model is a schematic description or diagram of a system, theory, or phenomenon related to education that accounts for its known or implied properties. It helps make sense of research, theories, and practices surrounding educational and organizational change, and allows us to visualize the big picture of change by breaking it down into more manageable parts.

The **Change Agent Model**, also referred to as the Meaning of Educational Change Model (Fullan & Stiegelbauer, 1991), says that building coalitions is the key to successful change. These coalitions should be built, with other change agents, both within and between groups of stakeholders. The change agent must find the best way to reach out to others, determine areas of common interest among and between stakeholders, and decide on the best means to move forward.

The Change Agent Model focuses on the individual stakeholders taking part in the change process. This model identifies and describes the different types of stakeholders—including student affairs staff, faculty, and students—that serve as change agents for institutions of higher education. This framework is the only one that discusses individual change agents in educational settings according to their characteristics and analyzes how these characteristics affect change.

One particularly important point this model makes is that change is more easily achieved when faculty members are included, since the faculty is a natural catalyst for change. In addition, there may be a need to expand the traditional definition of teacher beyond classroom instructor to include student affairs staff members (Harvey-Smith, 2003). This makes sense, considering that faculty and student affairs staff have more contact with students on a day-to-day basis than do other administrators, boards of trustees, and government officials. If the faculty and student services teams are not in favor of the change or resist it, then the change is not going to happen.

The **Change Process Model**, also known as the Change Agent's Guide Model, focuses on the problem to be changed. This model looks at the innovation as a process and examines each stage of that process. The Change Process Model maps out a series of phases that drive the momentum from the initial stage at which intended adopters come to care about an issue to the much later stage at which they bring about improvements. This framework helps the change agent pay attention to "crisis" areas of the innovation. Not all adopters go through the stages in the same order; some have to repeat a stage.

The **Resistance to Change Model**, also known as the Strategies for Planned Change Model (Zaltman & Duncan, 1977), examines ways in which change can be resisted and provides guidance on minimizing the resistance. This model suggests that change agents must first understand the barriers to change before they can develop strategies for overcoming opposition. The model groups potential barriers as cultural, social, organizational, or psychological. An understanding of resistance to change can lead to a better understanding of the system and is key to whether the change will occur.

The Resistance to Change Model can be useful to the change agent because it explores change from the opposite perspective of most other models. By focusing attention on factors that create barriers to change, it helps the change agent recognize obstacles as they arise and even to address underlying issues before they arise.

The **Systems Model** reaffirms that change agents need to be aware of all stakeholders and constituents likely to be affected by change. This model views systemic change as a holistic approach that change agents should endeavor to adopt when implementing change. The Systems Model calls for ensuring that a critical mass of coordinated innovations is in place and addressing stakeholders' needs by considering how these parts interrelate to form the system in which they are intended to function.

To fully understand systemic change, potential change agents must first be able to distinguish "systemic" from "systematic." Systemic change is often called a paradigm shift. This type of change often entails replacing the whole thing (Reigeluth & Garfinkle, 1994). Systematic, piecemeal change is often called tinkering. It entails modifying something or fixing a part of it.

Systemic change advocates focus on the fact that when one change is made in a system, it affects related parts and causes other changes. Systemic change also recognizes the role of power and leadership in any changing system.

These models are theories that allow us to make some fairly accurate predictions about how change occurs in educational institutions. Each model was crafted from reasonable assumptions and built on research findings. Each model likely applies best to support particular types of changes in particular types of institutions. We must keep in mind that no two educational institutions are exactly alike and thus no single strategy or model for change is appropriate for all institutions. Nonetheless, these models are powerful tools for individuals who are managing change because each allows change agents to benefit from insight about the structure of systems within an institution and their relationship to change.

Having an abundance of models from which to choose, however, can make it even harder for educational leaders to get the process going. Too much reading and studying about educational change can lead to information overload. Information overload can cause stakeholders to get bogged down by thinking too much about the process of change. It is often difficult for them to "think outside the box." The only kind of educational system they know is what they have experienced. Thus, their proposed solutions are piecemeal, despite the rhetoric of systemic change. Also, it is extremely difficult for people attempting to change education to immediately make change happen or to anticipate when change will occur, based on their decisions and plans.

CONCLUSION

The change process is both evolutionary and complex (Fullan, 1999). Some intended adopters resist change because it calls for them to rework or redefine a process they may be very comfortable with. However, change is needed in educational institutions to successfully deal with the issues facing them in the 21st century and beyond (Fullan, 1999). Fundamental to effecting change in an organization are questions such as: Who decides what will change? When will change take place?

As stated earlier, in educational institutions anyone in the stake-holding groups can communicate the need for change. However, not all situations may result in the type of change anticipated. Sometimes change in one aspect of the learning environment may precipitate changes in other areas. Conversely, change in some areas may not translate into change in the next area—especially in systems that still divide service functions from instructional functions.

Leaders more often than not are change agents in educational institutions. Even if the institution is highly decentralized, a collaborative approach to change will generally lead to greater acceptance of the change (Ellsworth, 2000). Change that is orchestrated from the top and imposed on individuals at the bottom is likely to be resisted. To reduce resistance, the change should be communicated at all levels so individuals will see the need and benefits and have some ownership of the change process.

REFERENCES

Ellsworth, J. B. (2000). *Surviving change: A survey of educational change models.* Syracuse, NY: ERIC Clearinghouse on Information and Technology.

Fullan, M. (1999). *Change forces: The sequel.* Philadelphia: Falmer Press.

Fullan, M., & Stiegelbauer, S. (1991). *The new meaning of educational change.* New York: Teachers College Press.

Harvey-Smith, A. B. (2003). *The adoption of the learning paradigm in student affairs divisions in Vanguard community colleges.* Unpublished doctoral dissertation, University of Maryland, College Park.

Merriam-Webster Online Dictionary. (2004). Retrieved June 2, 2004, from http://www.m-w.com/

Reigeluth, C., & Garfinkle, R. (1994). *Systemic change in education.* Englewood Cliffs, NJ: Educational Technology Publications.

Walton, M. (1986). *The Deming management method.* New York: Berkley Publishing Group.

Zaltman, G., & Duncan, R. (1977). *Strategies for planned change.* New York: John Wiley and Sons.

CHAPTER 5

Diffusion of Innovations in Student Affairs: A Mechanism for Understanding Change

Hanne Mawhinney and Alicia B. Harvey-Smith

"Everything is in a constant process of discovery and creating."

—MARGARET WHEATLEY & MYRON KELLNER-ROGERS

INTRODUCTION

The challenges of sustaining momentum in learning organizations are well known to anyone who has ever tried to make systemic change. Indeed, Peter Senge and his colleagues (1999) have documented the prevalence of the problem of diffusing innovative practice—that is, communicating an innovation over time among members of a social system (Rogers, 1995, 2003). Writing in *The Dance of Change*, Senge and colleagues describe the isolation, competitiveness, and distrust that pose serious challenges to efforts to sustain a change. If that change is an innovation, then diffusion depends on widespread knowledge dissemination.

The evidence of the diffusion of innovations that Everett Rogers, the eminent theorist of innovation diffusion, and others have accumulated offers lessons for those charged with overcoming the challenges of organizational change. In this chapter, we focus on how leaders can use these lessons to sustain the momentum for innovation by fostering the conditions that enhance the diffusion of innovations, and we show how diffusion worked at two community colleges. Rogers' model of innovation diffusion offers important insights into the ways in which organizational leaders can overcome these challenges. He focuses on the characteristics of innovation, how it is communicated, the decision process and its timing, the innovativeness of adopters, and qualities of the social system and organization.

ROGERS' DIFFUSION MODEL

Today many innovations are technological; still, they involve actions that reduce the uncertainty of achieving desired outcomes. Rogers believes that it is important to consider the characteristics of an innovation that determine its rate of adoption. He lists five characteristics that can influence adoption rates:

1. Relative advantage—The perceptions of the relative advantage of one innovation over others
2. Compatibility—The degree to which an innovation is perceived by potential adopters as consistent with their values, experiences, and needs
3. Complexity—How difficult an innovation is to understand and use
4. Trialability—The perception that an innovation can be tried out without fully committing to its adoption
5. Observability—The extent to which an innovation can be easily observed

Innovations that are perceived by potential adopters as having greater relative advantage, compatibility, trialability, and observability and less complexity will be adopted more rapidly than other innovations (Rogers, 1995, pp. 15-16).

It is also important to consider that how individuals view an innovation may be influenced by the ways that they have modified its use to their advantage. Innovators often modify an innovation, and indeed there is evidence that an innovation diffuses more rapidly when it can be reinvented and that this process enhances its sustainability.

Communication Channels

A communication channel is the means by which messages get from one individual to another. The channels through which innovations are communicated influence adoption of innovations. Rogers views diffusion as a social process of spreading an innovation that occurs when people talk to other people about their adoption decisions. He argues that "mass media channels are more effective in creating initial knowledge of innovations, whereas interpersonal channels are more effective in forming and changing attitudes toward a new idea, and thus in influencing the decision to adopt or reject a new idea" (2002, p. 990).

Mass media channels include radio, television, and newspapers. Rogers (2003) points out that mass media have the advantage of reaching a large audience rapidly, creating knowledge, spreading information, and changing weakly held attitudes. In contrast, when there is a need to form and change strongly held attitudes, interpersonal channels involving face-to-face exchanges between individuals are more effective. Interpersonal communications enable individuals to obtain clarification or additional information from others in ways that overcome barriers of selective exposure, perception, and retention.

Innovation-Decision Process

Rogers claims that the innovation-decision process passes through five stages: knowledge, persuasion, decision, implementation, and, finally, confirmation (2003, p. 169). Knowledge of the innovation occurs when an individual or decision-making body is exposed to an innovation and comes to understand how it functions. This is far from a simple process. Individuals tend to pay attention to communication about innovations that are consistent with their attitudes and beliefs; people do not commonly seek out messages about an innovation unless they feel that it is relevant to their needs.

The persuasion stage occurs when an individual forms a favorable or unfavorable attitude to the innovation. At this stage, individuals typically seek social reinforcement of their perceptions of the innovation from other individuals. They seek opinions about the advantages and disadvantages of the innovation for their situation.

Subsequently, decisions are made to adopt or reject the innovation. Adoption implies that a decision has been made to make full use of an innovation, and rejection implies that it will not be put to use. However, most individuals do not fully adopt an innovation without first trying it out, often in a small-scale trial. Indeed, recognition that innovations that can be tried are more likely to be adopted has led to the development of methods to facilitate the trial of innovations. Moreover, trials by peers, or even demonstrations of the innovation, have some credibility to potential adopters.

Implementation occurs when the idea is put into use. At this stage, there is still uncertainty about the expected consequences of adoption. Individuals want to know where they can obtain the innovation, how to use it, what kinds of operational problems could be encountered, and how they can be solved. The implementation stage is particularly problematic in organizational adoption of an innovation. The individuals implementing an innovation may not be those who adopted it. It is likely that implementation will occur over a considerable period of time, eventually reaching a point where a new idea becomes institutionalized into the regular organizational practices.

Innovation-decision making may also involve a confirmation process in which individuals seek reinforcement of the decision that they have made. They may even reverse the decision if they receive conflicting messages about the innovation.

Discontinuance of an innovation is not uncommon. Innovations often are replaced by new ideas; indeed, one of the concerns of many students of educational innovations is that new ideas crowd out previous innovations at a rate that creates chaos rather than the intended reform. Decisions to reject an innovation may also be influenced by dissatisfaction or disenchantment with its performance or its outcomes or the demands it makes for resources.

Adopter Categories

In Rogers' model, innovations are diffused over time in social systems. He defines innovativeness as the degree to which an individual or group is relatively earlier in adopting new ideas than other members of a social system; he then groups adopters into five categories, based on their innovativeness: innovators, early adopters, early majority, late majority, and laggards (Rogers, 1995, p. 22). Innovators are the first 2.5% of individuals in a system to adopt an innovation (Rogers, 1995, p. 262). They are interested in new ideas and are more likely to go outside local peer networks to seek those ideas. Although innovators may not be well respected by other members of a local system, they play an important role in launching new ideas in the system and therefore in importing outside innovations (Rogers, 1995, p. 283).

Early adopters represent the next 13.3 % to adopt an innovation (Rogers, 1995, p. 262). These individuals are more integrated into local systems than are the more venturesome innovators. Knowing that their peers respect them, early adopters typically try to make judicious innovation decisions. When they adopt an innovation, they help to trigger the adoption by a critical mass of individuals.

The early majority of adopters consists of the next 34% of individuals who adopt an innovation (Rogers, 1995, p. 262). Rogers observes that these individuals may deliberate for some time before completely adopting a new idea (Rogers, 1995, p. 284).

The late majority, representing 34% of the system actors, are those individuals who adopt the innovation just after the average number of a system (Rogers, 1995, p. 262). They are typically more skeptical and cautious in deciding to adopt, and do so only after most others in the system have already done so (Rogers, 1995, p. 284).

Laggards are the last 16% of individuals to adopt an innovation (Rogers, 1995, p. 262). Rogers argues that they only "accept a new idea when they are surrounded by peers who have already adopted and who are satisfied with the new idea" (2002, p. 991).

Social System

A central element of Rogers' (2003) model of innovation diffusion is the concept of the influence of the social system in which it occurs. The social system "constitutes the boundary within which an innovation diffuses" (Rogers, 2003, p. 24). Many aspects of social systems influence innovation diffusion: social structure, norms, the roles of opinion leaders and change agents, the types of innovation decisions that are made, and the consequences of innovation and change within a social system.

Rogers defines social structure as "the patterned arrangements of the units in a system . . . [that give] regularity and stability to human behavior in a system" (2003, p. 24). For example, bureaucratic organizations, consisting of hierarchical positions, establish patterns of social relationships among members that predict direction and flow of information. There are also informal networks linking system members.

Internal organizational structural characteristics that influence innovation diffusion in organizations include the extent of centralization of power and control in the hands of a few individuals, the complexity of the collective organizational capacity for knowledge (based on the degree to which individuals possess relatively high levels of expertise), the extent of organizational formalization through emphasis on rules and procedures, the degree to which units in the organization are interconnected and linked through interpersonal networks, and the extent to which the organization has available uncommitted resources (or slack). Rogers reports "each of these organizational variables may be related to innovation in one direction during the initiation phases of the innovation process, and in the opposite direction during the implementation phases" (2003, pp. 412-413).

According to Rogers, norms are established behavior patterns for the members of a social system. Norms define a range of tolerable behavior and serve as a guide or standard for the behavior of members of a social system. The norms of a system tell individuals what behavior they are expected to perform (Rogers, 2003, p. 26).

Opinion leaders influence others' "attitudes or overt behavior informally in a desired way with relative frequency" (Rogers, 2003, p. 27).

Opinion leadership is informally earned based on an individual's "technical competence, social accessibility, and conformity to the system's norms" (Rogers, 2003, p. 27). Unlike opinion leaders, change agents may come from agencies external to an organization. Typically, they are charged with the task of influencing innovation decisions. Change agents often use opinion leaders to support their diffusion activities.

Decisions can be optional and made by individuals, they can be collective, or authorities can make them. The diffusion of innovations generally occurs most rapidly under authority types of decisions, although these decisions may also be circumvented.

MEETING THE CHALLENGES OF DIFFUSION OF THE LEARNING PARADIGM IN STUDENT AFFAIRS

How difficult is it for innovations like the ideas of the learning paradigm to become diffused? What are the consequences of efforts to institutionalize this idea into the practices of student affairs divisions? Anyone considering adopting the learning college principle has these questions.

We can learn about the diffusion of complex innovations such as the learning paradigm from the qualitative case studies that Alicia B. Harvey-Smith (2003) undertook. Harvey-Smith examined the diffusion of the learning paradigm at two community colleges, which she calls Southwest Community College (SCC) and North Community College (NCC).

Many of the elements of an innovation that Rogers considers important to diffusion (1995, 2003) were evident when the student affairs divisions at SCC and NCC adopted the learning paradigm as a result of mounting dissatisfaction with student performance.

> At SCC, implementation of the learning paradigm was a
> response to growing frustration with student perform-
> ance, particularly that of Black and Hispanic students,
> who, according to institutional data, had significantly

lower success rates than other demographic groups (Harvey-Smith, 2003).

At NCC, the implementation of the learning paradigm resulted in new ways of thinking about student affairs practices and led to new approaches to support student learning outside of the classroom. Over time, NCC saw that the shifts in practices furthered the division's strategic emphasis on providing both access and success opportunities in a systematic way. Moreover, the integration of the learning paradigm and its related practices and processes provided focus and streamlined initiatives to enhance student learning (Harvey-Smith, 2003).

The learning paradigm was implemented in the student affairs divisions of these two institutions more rapidly than in other units; division members felt it was a natural extension of student affairs work and a necessary change. The learning paradigm transformed organizational structures, business practices, initiatives, and approaches supporting student learning. The innovation affected institutional governance as the structures adjusted to provide greater opportunity in decision making for student affairs. At NCC, a student affairs administrator described the change and restructuring:

The innovation made us rethink our structure to determine if it was the right one for our students. We eventually began to regroup functions differently and streamline processes. This new approach to doing business was a major outcome of the adoption/change process. (Harvey-Smith, 2003)

Communicating the Learning Paradigm in Student Affairs Divisions

In the student affairs divisions at SCC and NCC, those leading institutional transformation worked hard to communicate information regarding the adoption/change process. They used a variety of mechanisms such as formal and informal channels, e-mails, websites, newsletters, and memoranda to communicate the need for change and to solicit feedback in order to arrive at mutual understanding. Both divisions used extensive interpersonal channels, described by Rogers as the most effective in influencing change decisions, to convince community members of the value of the innovation of the learning paradigm.

At SCC, the process of communicating was hindered at first by the organizational structure of student affairs. Individuals considered the structure disjointed, with a mixed matrix configuration and dotted reporting lines. The configuration prohibited effective communication and did not provide "real" authority to lead the student affairs division in a comprehensive manner:

> Communicating within this structure was complicated, to say the least. We consistently looked for ways to provide information, unsuccessfully." Communication within the division was improved when efforts were consolidated and re-centralized. The re-centralization aided in providing increased focus to the programs and services that were previously viewed as disconnected or too removed from student affairs. (Harvey-Smith, 2003)

Institution leaders decided that additional effort would be directed at effective communication as innovations and initiatives are launched. The change in structure greatly contributed to the success of the adoption/change process. Consolidating, recentralizing, and focusing programs and services that had been disjointed and complicated by a mixed-matrix configuration improved communication.

At NCC, the communication challenge was to drive messages deeper into the organization on a consistent level. Oral communication of the innovation, new ideas, and initiatives took the form of utilizing consultants, focus groups, forums, and dialogues. Written communication took the form of e-mails, websites, newsletters, and memoranda. A senior student affairs administrator had this to say about the communication challenge:

> We worked hard to communicate. Our leadership team consistently sought input and allowed us to weigh in on the value of change. Even though many times the message was sent and received, many chose to hear only what they wanted and not fully buy in. (Harvey-Smith, 2003)

The communication styles of SCC's president and the senior student affairs officer and NCC's vice president positively influenced the adoption/change process and helped community members make meaning of change.

An observer at NCC noted:

> How communication happened made a real difference and was really important to the speed at which we changed, not just within the many committees but also with all the stakeholders all across the college. We wanted people talking about it and not to be surprised. In some cases, we experienced a communication breakdown, or there wasn't sufficient communication, and that always affected buy-in and slowed us down. (Harvey-Smith, 2003)

At both colleges, better communication processes that increased and improved collaborations and partnerships, particularly between student affairs and academic affairs, drove the need for change deeper into the organization and redefined processes.

Illuminating many of the initiatives and innovative concepts that were in development in student affairs at SCC prior to the formal adoption/change process was one strategy used to bridge the gap between academic affairs and student affairs as greater input was sought from core faculty members.

Timing the Adoption of the Learning Paradigm

The experience of the student affairs divisions in SCC and NCC offers insights into timing the adoption of the learning paradigm. The rate of adoption at both colleges was influenced by research completed prior to implementing the learning paradigm, the perceived fit of the paradigm with the philosophy, the vision and mission of student affairs, and the leadership. At SCC, a senior administrator in student affairs reflected on the time and rate of adoption of the new paradigm in this way:

> The student affairs division felt compelled to make changes to better support the learning of students. We wanted to improve our results. After conducting some research, we decided the learning paradigm made sense; and we moved rather quickly to implement. Technology also served to accelerate our efforts. (Harvey-Smith, 2003)

Individuals at SCC noted the speed at which change occurred in student affairs and the concern that it was viewed at times as "too quick" (Harvey-Smith, 2003). A change of administration and a new technology system sped up the adoption of the learning paradigm. One observer at SCC said, "Technology has served a key role in accelerating change and the adoption of new practices in student services; it has been all forward momentum" (Harvey-Smith, 2003). The provost at SCC noted that the change in leadership increased the adoption of new practices and processes: "Changes in leadership and approaching change holistically helped our institution to move" (Harvey-Smith, 2003).

Eventually, concern about the rapidity of the changes led the SCC student affairs division to "slow down to speed up" (Harvey-Smith, 2003), a plan to slow the process of change down enough to solicit and incorporate wider input from a larger constituency prior to implementing change, thus leading to a more comprehensive and permanent institutional impact.

In contrast, NCC adopted change at the institutional level more slowly. Even so, the innovation-decision process was expedited in student affairs by the centralization and alignment of related functions. The process of moving from first knowledge of the learning paradigm to adopting it as a practice allowed the division to benefit from the diverse talents of its staff by better enabling cross-training. One individual at NCC observed:

> Time was taken to explore and understand the paradigm. It didn't take us much time to know it could provide us a foundation for change and be a basis for us to work differently as a team, learning from each other. We grouped like functions first, before anywhere else at the college. The approach was purely from a student learning, student success perspective. The major reason retention services was formed was to take advantage of the knowledge and expertise of a wide variety of individuals and departments. (Harvey-Smith, 2003)

MEETING THE CHALLENGE OF INNOVATION DIFFUSION

In a chapter on diffusion in *The Dance of Change*, Senge and his colleagues (1999) observed, "High-leverage strategies for dealing with this challenge concentrate on building the different dimensions of an organization's capacity to diffuse innovative practices: coaching capacity, permeability of boundaries, information infrastructure, and a learning culture and infrastructure." They identify several strategies to address these organizational dimensions that we have found supported by the focus on opinion leaders, idea champions and change agents, diffusion networks, and critical mass of adopters described in the diffusion model developed by Rogers (1995, 2003) and evident in the diffusion of the learning paradigm at SCC and NCC.

Opinion Leaders

Rogers (2003) argues that opinion leaders influence community members to move them to adopt or reject an innovation. Opinion leaders were influential in the diffusion of the learning paradigm at both SCC and NCC.

At SCC, the early grants leadership teams helped to move the dialogue of learning and change forward. The institutional leadership insisted on driving the dialogue deeper into the organization; the Learning-Centered Initiative leadership team, which was cochaired by the senior student affairs administrator with membership including faculty and staff, exerted tremendous influence in shaping the attitudes and behavior of the community. The student services vice president and work groups consisting of student services staff and faculty initiated discussions on the adoption of new approaches in advising that expanded opportunities for collaborations. The senior student affairs administrator at SCC was an opinion leader and is described by one respondent as "Focused on outcomes and able to get a lot done due to his leadership and influence" (Harvey-Smith, 2003). His long-time standing at the institution earned him a high level of respect and credibility.

At NCC, primary opinion leadership came from the middle to upper levels of leadership in the student affairs division.

Individuals involved in the diffusion process at NCC said seeding new ideas as a team and being encouraged to take risks by the division leadership increased the rate at which change was accepted and adopted. The process of funding innovation was also described as being influenced by the division's long-time opinion leaders who have, over time, built trust and credibility.

Respondents said informal conversations, e-mails, and engagement that involved peers and institutional leaders helped the process along. The student affairs leadership team was instrumental in driving dialogue and exchange throughout the organization.

Idea Champions

Rogers (2003) argues that idea champions may create connections among individuals in an organization and play crucial roles in organizational innovativeness. Research shows that without their support, new ideas have little chance of adoption.

We found that at SCC, the champions of the idea of the learning paradigm were the innovators or the "early visionaries" who led initial efforts and involvement in research, grants, and involvement in the Learning-Centered Initiative. The president and senior-level administrators were active innovators throughout the process.

Change Agents

At both SCC and NCC, change agents accelerated the adoption/change process in student affairs by pushing for change and adoption of the learning paradigm (Rogers, 1995, 2003). At NCC, leaders were change agents and assertively moved stakeholders toward adoption/change as the learning paradigm was researched, initiated, and implemented. The change agents in the organization partnered effectively with the opinion leaders to diffuse the learning paradigm throughout the student affairs division.

The NCC student affairs leadership team served as change agents throughout the adoption process. A long-time NCC student affairs senior staff person described the role of change agent as played by individuals on the leadership team: "We saw ourselves as having the responsibility of making the right type of change happen. The type of change that made us a better division and that made students make the right connections was important to us" (Harvey-Smith, 2003).

Another staff person observed, "We had opinions, and some of them differed; but what we agreed on was the need to change how we were engaging students and how they were experiencing our institution" (Harvey-Smith, 2003).

At SCC, leaders who defined themselves and their work as change-enabling accelerated the adoption/change process. The adoption/change process in student affairs at SCC was improved and the rate of adoption increased by the number of individuals involved early on, who brought others along. The opinion leaders and change agents were also early adopters of change and new ideas, and they served as role models. They played important roles in what Rogers calls diffusion networks and in initiating the dynamics that could lead to a critical mass of individuals adopting the learning paradigm.

Diffusion Networks and Critical Mass

Rogers suggests that interpersonal networks exert important influences on individuals' decisions to adopt innovations.

Personal networks consist of those "interconnected individuals who are linked by patterned communication flows to a given individual" (Rogers, 2003, p. 363). Rogers argues that personal networks that are more open to an individual's environment play a more important role in the diffusion of innovations than those that disregard this element.

Networks provide a degree of structure and stability to these processes. Communication structure reflects the patterns of communication flow in a system. Rogers suggests that this structure consists of cliques within a system and the network connections among them that are provided by bridges and liaisons. He also suggests that interpersonal communication drives the diffusion process by creating a critical mass of adopters, when enough individuals in a system have adopted an innovation so that its further diffusion becomes self-sustaining.

At SCC and NCC, opinion leaders and change agents played important roles in reaching critical mass.

At SCC, although it was not clear whether the point of critical mass had been reached, several respondents felt they continued to progress in that direction and used terms such as "tipping point" and "cusp of transformation" to describe their current stage (Harvey-Smith, 2003). Another respondent, a long-time faculty member, noted that SCC is also reaching critical mass in the number of faculty who are part of the collaborations and partnerships that emerged from the adoption of the learning paradigm and the learning focus of student affairs.

At NCC, crucial to the implementation and sustainability of innovation and change in student affairs were the gains made in achieving critical mass. This self-sustaining ability was the goal of the division and increased due to the influence of stakeholders who were part of the process from the beginning as opinion leaders and change agents.

> Efforts to build a critical mass institutionally and divisionally at NCC were extensive and included measures to gain support for change efforts. According to respondents at NCC, the institution had not reached critical mass at the time of the study in terms of full change implementation but was moving quickly in that direction, with the rate of adoption having increased significantly within the last year (Harvey-Smith, 2003).

Individuals at NCC described the critical mass in the student affairs division and the synergy that was created as both self-sustaining and crucial to their transformation. Respondents credited the high level of support and critical mass in student affairs to the philosophical compatibility of the learning paradigm and the guiding principles of student personnel work. The learning paradigm and related changes were described as "making sense" and "just feeling right" by several members of the student affairs staff (Harvey-Smith, 2003).

Figure 1: Increasing Organizational Capacity for Innovation Diffusion

Senge and his colleagues (1999) argued that the most effective diffusion occurs when people have opportunities to cross traditional boundaries to work with one another. In this chapter, we have shown why it is important that organizations increase their capacity for innovation diffusion. The following 10 considerations to take into account come from our examination of Rogers' model of innovation diffusion and our discussion of efforts of individuals in student affairs divisions at Southwest Community College and Northern Community College to diffuse the learning paradigm.

1. Understand the attributes of the innovation, and consider how organizational members will perceive them. Will they see it as having a relative advantage? As compatible with their values? Does the organization have the resources to deal with innovational complexity? Can the innovation be tried out? Can it be modeled and observed?

2. What is the rate at which an innovation is likely to be adopted by members of the organization? Who are the innovators in the organization, and how can their venturesomeness be tapped? Who are likely to be early adopters, and how can the respect in which they are held be used to support diffusion of the innovation? What kinds of information will help the early majority deliberate on the innovation? How can system norms be framed so they will overcome the skepticism of the late majority? How can the late adopters be reassured?

3. Consider the communication channels that provide the appropriate information to organizational members. How can mass media channels be used to reach a large audience rapidly, to create knowledge and spread information, and to change weakly held attitudes? How can interpersonal channels be used to increase the two-way exchange of information among individuals in order to change strongly held attitudes?

(Continued on next page)

Figure 1: (Continued from page 85)

4. Consider the nature of the innovation-decision process. How can individuals gain knowledge of the questions that are raised by the innovation, such as what it is, how it works, and why it works? How can individuals be persuaded? How will the perceived characteristics of the innovation influence their attitude? What considerations must be taken into account in deciding to adopt or reject the innovation? How can questions raised in implementing the innovation be answered? Where can it be obtained? How is it to be used? What operational problems will be encountered? How much reinvention is possible with the innovation? How much faster will this make the adoption process? How much more sustainability will be possible, and how will this help institutionalize the innovation? What kinds of supports for confirmation are needed? Is it possible that the innovation will be discontinued? If so, will it be replaced by another innovation? Will individuals become disenchanted with it?

5. Understand the communications networks involved in the diffusion of the innovation. What is the structure of who relays messages to whom?

6. Consider the importance of the opinion leaders. Who has greater exposure to mass media? Who has extensive interpersonal networks in the system? Whose orientation to innovativeness matches that of the organization? Who is widely respected by organizational members?

7. Consider the nature of diffusion networks associated with the innovation. What is the communication structure or the patterned communication flow? What cliques have formed through personal communication networks and to what extent are these based on interlocking patterns of communication? Whose personal networks are open? How can weak ties formed through contacts made in radial networks be fostered? How can these weak ties be strengthened?

(Continued on next page)

Figure 1: (Continued from page 86)

8. Understand the importance of the critical mass in the diffusion of innovations. How can interactive communication technologies be used to support the adoption of the innovation? How can exchange systems that allow mutual discourse be used in the diffusion process? What is the tipping point for critical mass? Is it possible that a critical mass of individuals will decide to discontinue the innovation? What individual thresholds for adoption are associated with the innovation? Who are the highly respected individuals that should be targeted to help diffuse the innovation? Which innovators are likely to adopt the innovation? What are the incentives for adoption?

9. Consider who are possible change agents. Will they make the effort needed to engage with organizational members? Is the diffusion program compatible with the needs of the individuals adopting the innovation?

10. Consider organizational variables. What is the structure of the organization? Look at characteristics such as centralization, complexity, formalization, interconnectedness, organizational slack, and size. What is the attitude of organizational leaders toward the innovation? Who are the champions of the innovation? What are the initiation and implementation stages through which the innovation must pass to become institutionalized?

CONCLUSION

Repeatedly, individuals involved in the change process at both NCC and SCC noted that all systems and practices in the divisions facilitated change. At NCC, the social system responded cohesively to address challenges and to accomplish the goals of fully adopting the learning paradigm and moving the institution from one that merely provides access to one that enhances the success of all its learners. Cultural support and support in the form of directing resources and changing the architecture to align functions comprehensively allowed NCC to philosophically and strategically coordinate its systems. A member of the student affairs leadership team at NCC reflected:

> The environment at NCC, particularly in student affairs, encouraged creativity and the risk taking through innovation. The college leadership through governance and establishment of new councils provided us flexibility. The social system was supportive of leadership that emerged from student affairs. (Harvey-Smith, 2003)

Each institution, at some level, achieved that which it aimed to accomplish. The overall performance, success, engagement, and involvement of students at both sites improved.

REFERENCES

Harvey-Smith, A. B. (2003). *The adoption of the learning paradigm in student affairs divisions in Vanguard community colleges.* Unpublished doctoral dissertation, University of Maryland, College Park.

Rogers, E. M. (1962). *Diffusion of innovations.* New York: Free Press.

Rogers, E. M. (1995). *Diffusion of innovations* (4th ed.). New York: Free Press.

Rogers, E. M. (2002). Diffusion of preventative innovations. *Addictive Behaviors, 27,* 989-993.

Rogers, E. M. (2003). *Diffusion of innovations* (5th ed.). New York: Free Press.

Senge, P., Kliner, A., Roberts, C., Ross, R., Roth, G., & Smith, B. (1999). *The dance of change: The challenges to sustaining momentum in learning organizations.* New York: Doubleday/Currency.

CHAPTER 6

The Evolving Role of Student Affairs in Learning Organizations

Alicia B. Harvey-Smith

"Everything participates in the creation and evolution of its neighbors."

—MARGARET WHEATLEY & MYRON KELLNER-ROGERS

INTRODUCTION

As a result of recent research on student affairs divisions in the 21st-century learning college movement, student affairs practices are shifting on several levels. These shifts are structural and philosophical; they involve the emergence of a new and shared language; they demonstrate extensive efforts to integrate (Harvey-Smith, 2003). Not surprisingly, these shifts involve expanded partnerships and a greater examination of ingrained perspectives regarding teaching and learning, reflect an alignment of practice with learning principles, and result in a redefinition of the role of student development.

Noting restrictive frameworks in the higher education landscape, O'Banion (1997) emphasized the need for higher education to examine its practices and "overhaul its outdated traditional framework" (p. 1). This also holds true for student affairs organizations. As colleges continue to develop environments that better support learning, it is appropriate that student affairs personnel assume a leading role.

Since their earliest days, student affairs divisions have contributed consistently to student learning and academic success. Now, in response to the learning college movement, student affairs professionals will be expected to take an even more visible and proactive role. Student services functions may need to be strategically redesigned to promote learning and self-reflection.

At present, the most frequent role of student affairs divisions can best be described as traditional, complete with artificial divides that separate them from academic units. Often, they operate independently of other institutional areas. In contrast, the emerging role of student affairs in learning organizations is one of integration and connectivity with the college; it also includes clearer ties and partnerships between student affairs and academic and instructional divisions.

TRADITIONAL TO EXPANSIVE ROLE

Two of the most enduring concepts in the student affairs tradition are commitment to the development of the whole person and enhancement of the academic mission. As student affairs divisions continue to develop programs to enhance student learning, how they align practices in support of the learning paradigm is critical. This alignment with the learning paradigm seems a natural alliance, as student development practices have a fundamental orientation toward change and holistic learning.

However, the traditional separations among academic departments, lack of faculty participation and collaboration, staffing turnover in entry-level student affairs positions, ineffective budget and reporting structures, and poor institutional communication often limit the effectiveness of operations and ultimately harm learners. A partnership model, which is characterized by extensive collaborations and connections among student affairs professionals, faculty, and academic administrators, is one solution.

Banta and Kuh (1998) urged increased collaboration between academic affairs and student affairs, particularly in the area of college assessment. During the past two decades, research has shown that improving the undergraduate experience requires the collaboration of academic and student affairs divisions, the two areas most engaged with students. Institutional improvement depends on getting the best information about where student learning occurs and how it can be enhanced. The complete picture of student learning cannot be taken without academic affairs and student affairs working together.

No longer are student affairs divisions considered supplemental partners in the learning process. Instead, they are recognized as full partners in authentic learning organizations. Barr and Tagg (1995) cited the importance of the entire educational system's supporting the outcome of learning. The Joint Task Force on Student Learning (1998) in "Powerful Partnerships: A Shared Responsibility for Learning" provided support for extensive collaborations between student affairs and academic affairs to foster improved learning.

The success of student affairs in building partnerships with faculty in learning colleges will require such strategies as planning curriculum and assessment jointly, sharing academic and developmental roles such as advising, and communicating the goals of student development and its influence in the learning process college-wide. Coordinating learning experiences inside and outside the classroom, designing and administering learning outcome assessments, and using the results to improve the total student experience also will need to be part of the long-term student development plan for collaboration.

LEADING FROM THE CENTER

In order to create more inclusive and proactive environments, student affairs must continue to critically examine college policies and procedures and work to adjust them to meet the developmental needs of nontraditional students. To enhance learning for all students, student affairs divisions will need to implement processes that monitor progress, measure outcomes, and evaluate effectiveness of programs and services to students. These programs must promote student interaction and involvement with all aspects of student life and campus activities and serve all students, whether they attend day or evening, full time or part time, for credit or not for credit, or on weekdays or weekends. Included should be a career planning and placement program and educational planning, progress monitoring, and a prescription for appropriate intervention strategies, such as degree audits, early warning systems, and minimum academic progress checks.

Student affairs divisions will need to develop programs that identify contributions to learning and redirect the emphasis from administrative to educational concerns. They also will need to develop new models of how to create substantive learning. Those both outside and inside student affairs who hold traditional views will need to surrender them. This will require significant shifts in attitudes, orientation, and responsibilities.

The role that student affairs plays in developing and maintaining ongoing relationships with students is critical. If student learning and success are to be achieved, there is a greater need to extend these relationships and further examine the influence of out-of-class learning.

Authentic learning institutions continually assess and support the involvement of student affairs leadership for institution-wide change, as the compatibility of student affairs approaches and philosophies with learning-centered change gains recognition. Moreover, as the higher education landscape provides new opportunities to improve learning by establishing connected systems, institutions will better understand and implement learning-centered approaches (Harvey-Smith, 2003; James, 2002).

ASSESSMENT OF LEARNING

When student affairs divisions consider the adoption of the learning paradigm, they should think comprehensively about change and change processes, starting with a focus on the intended outcomes of change in terms of student learning results. It will be critical not to allow institutional history or old models to stifle the process.

Student affairs organizations should plan to request and share feedback openly and reach conclusions collaboratively. Institutional leaders must allow the process to evolve naturally, without attempting to control or manipulate its outcome. This will develop trust and commitment to achieving a unified direction.

Throughout the evolving process, those who challenge or are skeptical of the process should be encouraged to become involved. Widening the circle of involvement and including divergent voices improve the process.

INFLUENCES ON CHANGE

Leadership, communication, institutional support, organizational culture, and institutionalization significantly influence the evolution of student affairs in learning-centered organizations.

Leadership

Transformations will more likely take hold as a result of diverse leadership and the involvement of different constituencies. In learning-centered organizations, leadership can emerge from all areas. This recognition of diverse leadership is essential in providing a foundation for change implementation in student affairs and the larger community. Institutional leaders must support the voice of student affairs in deliberations about student learning. As leaders in student affairs, they need to advocate as change agents for the division's place at the table.

The leadership of the college president and chief student affairs officer deeply affects the transformation process. If the president publicly endorses involving the division in learning and granting it equal voice in all learning-focused deliberations, change will go deeper into the organization. One student affairs administrator reflected on lessons in leadership acquired in an evolving student affairs division:

> I think what I've learned more than leadership in the traditional sense is the importance of collaboration and understanding people's worlds. Even though we are all in higher education, there are real differences in perspectives. Good leaders must try to understand what people care about. What's important to you and what's important to me as a student affairs administrator, and what's

important to you as an admissions clerk, and what's important to you as a counselor or faculty member? You really need to take all of those perspectives into account and understand that what counts is that person's interaction with students, and the students' experience are most important. (Harvey-Smith, 2003)

Communication

Striving for authentic communication is a goal at transforming colleges; one tactic is to reverse the traditional approach to communicating. A president of a transforming institution described the goal for authentic communication in this manner:

Most people come up with an idea and then communicate, communicate, communicate, with no communication support. I think we have it backwards. You communicate, communicate, and communicate in order to generate the ideas first. In other words, communication and collaboration aren't authentic if it's to sell an idea. (Harvey-Smith, 2003)

Thus, institutions wishing to make lasting change must incorporate feedback from stakeholders to shape the change. Student affairs divisions in these environments aggressively create and maintain a continuous system of communication and feedback, arriving at a mutual understanding about their role. Communication includes high levels of openness and responsiveness, with many opportunities for input from stakeholders within and outside the student affairs division. Feedback mechanisms let stakeholders initiate and respond to proposed changes as well as broaden conversations about learning. The most frequently used feedback mechanisms include cross-functional learning dialogues, committees, roundtables, workshops, and surveys.

Institutional Support

As institutions seek to transform practice, a variety of support will be necessary in order to achieve change. For instance, institutional support in the form of financial and human capital, as well as opportunities for training and development, will prove essential. Transformation will also require shifts in governance and administrative structures to facilitate change, valuing the "voice" of student affairs and placing leadership for change in these divisions.

It is critical that institutions work to overcome historical and traditional challenges to become more learning-centered environments. Institutions may need to address such challenges as overcoming silos, lack of trust, lack of collaboration, naysayers who could halt the process, and people who might make decisions unilaterally.

Organizational Culture

One major mechanism for aiding community members in making meaning of changes taking place is organizational culture. Culture provides a filter through which information is processed. Student affairs cultures in transforming institutions influence community members' receptivity to change and how experiences are viewed and evaluated.

Transforming institutions have cultures that allow for greater risk taking and innovation. These cultures demonstrate greater levels of trust and reduce resistance to change. A senior faculty member at one institution had this observation concerning the culture's ability to break down faculty and administration suspicion of one another: "Our culture now recognizes and supports the good work emerging from student affairs. The differences in style and approach are readily accepted and appreciated" (Harvey-Smith, 2003).

Institutionalization

The institutionalization of change is probably one of the biggest challenges in the academy. Yet in authentic learning organizations, the institutionalization and assessment of changes are ongoing expectations, allowing innovation to be anchored in the culture. Such organizations expect new student affairs initiatives to be integrated into the life of the college and take steps to build coalitions in support of this planned integration. Within these environments, changes are fused into core competencies, strategic planning, and the ongoing processes and practices in student affairs.

Institutions may wish to plan for the integration of change as quality learning-centered initiatives are introduced and proven successful. At one transforming institution, the student affairs division institutionalized major change efforts in the form of a comprehensive advising system, significant collaborations with academic affairs, and the redesign of all business systems. A senior faculty member had this observation: "The initiatives that emerged from student affairs were designed with the end of institutionalization in mind. That's what makes change worth it. As a principle-based learning-centered organization, this is expected" (Harvey-Smith, 2003).

The institutionalization of change into the regular life of the campus, college, and culture, where it becomes a part of what is seen as normal practice, is an important goal of transforming learning-centered organizations. Developing and integrating a comprehensive delivery system that moves beyond customer service and from counting participation in events and activities to assessing the learning achieved as a result of engagement will be critical in this new role. The evolving role will culminate in the integration of this type of learning-centered change throughout the institution and its ongoing assessment. Figure 1 depicts one possible model of the evolving role of student affairs within the learning-centered architecture.

Figure 1: Process of transformed practice in student affairs.
Harvey-Smith, 2003

View student affairs as pedagogy

Use dissatisfaction to ignite innovation

Use literature as foundation for creation of new models

Make change understandable and authentic communication a goal

Gain input and feedback from diverse constituencies

Understand scope of influences impacting adoption/change to include leadership, communication, institutional support, institutional culture, and institutionalization

Invest appropriately in change

Set direction using students as compass

Be intentional about change and outcomes. Create seamless systems to support learning and assessment.

Match change with culture

Integrate to sustain

Ongoing assessment and evaluation of outcomes to build culture of evidence

CONCLUSION

The evolving role of student affairs will incorporate innovative processes that are broad-based, involving student affairs personnel, faculty, students, deans, department chairs, and other institutional leaders working together as partners, communicating from the onset of the change process.

The expanded role will be responsive and will allow opportunities throughout the process to review and discuss the literature, identify models of best practice, and focus on the goal of increasing understanding of change. As student affairs divisions embark on learning-centered change, learning expectations must be made explicit. Assessment rubrics will determine if, how, and when expected outcomes are achieved.

There are challenges and opportunities woven into the tapestry of organizational change, yet the complexity diminishes and challenges fade when approached strategically and comprehensively. Student affairs divisions in the 21st-century learning college will succeed or fail in their new role in large part as a result of their ability to develop and implement a plan that enhances student learning and success and documents the achievement of intended outcomes.

Moreover, the role of student affairs will be multifaceted. It will move student affairs organizations from traditional to expansive relationships and from supplemental to full and equal partners in the learning enterprise. It will shift student affairs from isolated to integrated and strategic planning, from reactive to proactive approaches, from counting to assessing, and from operating on the edge to leading from the center of the organization. It will influence how the community of learners makes meaning of and validates their experiences. This will allow new ways of understanding learning and approaching change to be introduced into the social system supporting transformation.

REFERENCES

Banta, T. W., & Kuh, D. K. (1998). A missing link in assessment: Collaboration between academic and student affairs professionals. *Change, 38*(6), 40-46.

Barr, R. B., & Tagg, J. (1995). From teaching to learning: A new paradigm for undergraduate education. *Change, 42*(7), 13-25.

Harvey-Smith, A. B. (2003). *The adoption of the learning paradigm in student affairs divisions in Vanguard community colleges.* Unpublished doctoral dissertation, University of Maryland, College Park.

James, T. (2002, June). No longer Cinderella: The future of student development services. Presentation given at the annual conference of the American Association of Community Colleges. Seattle, WA.

Joint Task Force on Student Learning. (1998). *Powerful partnerships: A shared responsibility for learning.* Washington, DC: American Association for Higher Education, American College Personnel Association, and National Association of Student Personnel Administrators.

O'Banion, T. (1997). *A learning college for the 21st century.* Phoenix, AZ: Oryx Press.

CHAPTER 7

From Theory to Practice: A Blueprint for Transformation Using Learning College Principles

Kim Poast, Alicia B. Harvey-Smith, Rashida Govan, and Mary Jean Rusnak

"We have stepped into a future that we can't even see."

—MARGARET WHEATLEY

INTRODUCTION

The future of student affairs within the evolving postsecondary landscape will require new approaches in response to complex challenges and rapidly changing institutional dynamics. As the role of student affairs continues to evolve, a blueprint for effective learning-centered change becomes critical and will demand change on many levels. Implementing learning-centered student affairs programs can be made unnecessarily complex if the paradigm and its principles are not fully understood. Such complexity can be reduced when institutional shifts in attitudes accompany shifts in practice.

This chapter offers a blueprint for change in student affairs by exploring each of the seven learning college principles and providing practical examples from student affairs divisions that have successfully implemented learning-centered changes in alignment with each of the principles. Strategies are provided on how to implement learning transformations in any college environment.

CREATE SUBSTANTIVE CHANGE IN INDIVIDUAL LEARNERS

O'Banion's (1997) first learning college principle is that a college should "create substantive change in individual learners" (p. 47). In order for this principle to be realized, it is important that the college have it embedded in the institutional culture. This principle's primary role is to encourage learners to develop new ways of "seeing, thinking, and doing...that lead to changed behavior" (O'Banion, 1997, p. 48). Pima Community College (PCC) provides an excellent example of this principle through its Student Medallion Leadership Institute.

PCC opened in 1970 in Tucson, Arizona. It reported an enrollment of 68,425 in fiscal year 2002-2003 at its six campuses (Pima Community College Student Profile, n.d.) with an ethnic breakdown composed of 52% White/non-Hispanic, 28.8% Hispanic, 3.8% African American/Black, 3.3% Native American, and 3% Asian/Pacific Islander students (National Center for Educational Statistics, n.d.). As of fall 2002, Pima Community College ranked as the eighth-largest multi-campus community college in the nation, offering courses in 62 program areas (Pima Community College Quick Facts, n.d.).

In 2001, PCC developed the Student Medallion Leadership Institute (SMLI). The program requires close collaboration between student affairs divisions, instructional teams, and community partners to "develop leaders by engaging them cognitively, as well as providing them with knowledge of society and opportunities to assess their progress" (Jennings, McCabe, & Strickland, 2004, p. 6).

The program has four major components: diversity appreciation, leadership, teamwork, and service learning. To participate, students must apply and commit to a rigorous program which includes the completion of two three-credit leadership development courses, participation in clubs/student organizations, attendance at student life functions, performance of service learning projects, and participation in diversity appreciation activities (Jennings, McCabe, & Strickland, 2004). Each activity completed by the student is assigned a point value that is tracked and maintained by each campus' student life program. A total of 2,500 points enables the student to wear an Institute medallion at graduation. In addition, students have a portfolio and an affidavit of accomplishments (in lieu of a transcript) (Jennings, McCabe, & Strickland, 2004). On completion of PCC's program, students who transfer to the University of Arizona may automatically enter its highly selective Blue Chip Leadership Program (Blue Chip Leadership Program at University of Arizona, n.d.).

The Student Medallion Leadership Institute has had over 150 students participate and has awarded approximately 28 medallions (M. McCabe, personal communication, July 2, 2004). The college reports several unexpected outcomes, including interest in replication of the program in other Arizona community colleges, staff and faculty participation in a statewide effort to support development of student leaders, and the success of PCC students transferring into the Blue Chip Leadership Program (Jennings, McCabe, & Strickland, 2004).

> Finally, inherent in the program is the constructivist philosophical paradigm that "experiences affect the perception of (and participation in) reality." Exposing students to opportunities and experiences that would not otherwise be available to them changes their perceptions of themselves, thus changing the way they view their relationship to the college and their communities at large (M. McCabe, personal communication, July 2, 2004).

ENGAGE LEARNERS IN THE LEARNING PROCESS AS FULL PARTNERS

O'Banion's (1997) second learning principle, which is to "engage learners as full partners in the learning process" (p. 47), relies on two key expectations for new learners: that learners are full partners in the creation and implementation of their learning experiences, and that learners will eventually assume primary responsibility for making their own educational choices. The college's responsibility is to provide students with tools, skills, and opportunities for experimentation, particularly for students who are unfamiliar with learning environments (O'Banion, 1997). New student orientation programs are an excellent way for institutions to provide these opportunities, and Moraine Valley Community College (MVCC) has set the standard for model orientation programs in community colleges.

MVCC, which opened in 1968, is located in the southwest suburbs of Cook County, Illinois. MVCC reported a fall 2004 enrollment of 16,077 with an ethnic background consisting of 78.2% White/non-Hispanic, 7.9% African American/Black, 9.7% Hispanic, 2.2% Asian/Pacific Islander, and 0.2% Native American students (Moraine Valley Community College Enrollment and Student Characteristics, n.d.). Approximately 30% of full-time and 60% of part-time students receive some type of financial aid (Moraine Valley Community College Enrollment and Student Characteristics, n.d.). MVCCC offers 106 degree and certificate programs serving 26 regional communities in Cook County (Moraine Valley Community College Enrollment and Student Characteristics, n.d.).

MVCC addressed the core value of engagement of learners as full partners by implementing a First Year Experience (FYE) program in 2000. The program acknowledges that a student's first year in college is a "critical period for academic adjustment and social integration" (Manley, Taylor, & Wright, 2003) and incorporates strategies to ensure academic success and continuous engagement in the college culture.

Upon admission, each full-time student is required to participate in the three components of the FYE program: college assessment and placement in reading, composition, and mathematics; new student orientation; and a one-credit student success course (COL-101, College: Changes, Challenges, Choices) (Manley, Taylor, & Wright, 2003).

MVCC utilizes the Computerized Assessment of Basic Reading, Writing and Math Skills (COMPASS") to ensure that students are appropriately placed in relevant courses. Rather than adopting a deficit model of assessment (i.e., testing into precollege courses is "bad" and testing into college-level courses is "good"), the college has changed its language in order to normalize precollege placement (i.e., language such as: "everyone tests into precollege courses, and if you score higher, that's great").

Following assessment, students participate in a half-day Student Orientation and Registration session (SOAR) facilitated by college counselors and academic advisers. SOAR provides students with information on college expectations, educational planning, a review of assessment placement, individualized assistance with course selection and semester planning, and an introduction to an online program that includes an assessment of orientation competencies as well as information regarding policies, procedures, and academic options (Dungy & Clements, 2003). From summer 2001 to summer 2003, participation in SOAR increased by 69% from 1,554 to 2,631 (Manley, Taylor, & Wright, 2003).

The hallmark of the FYE program is the one-credit COL 101 course designed to "enhance student development and learning and to improve student retention and academic success" (Dungy & Clements, 2003, p. 11). Faculty consist of teaching faculty, staff, and administrators who possess a master's degree and have completed a five-hour training session led by the assistant dean of student development, counseling faculty, and other COL-101 staff (Manley, Taylor, & Wright, 2003).

The curriculum includes career exploration, academic major selection, study skills strategies, stress and time management, developing awareness of self and college, and the development of a Master Academic Plan to guide the student through future academic choices (Manley, Taylor, & Wright, 2003).

Moraine Valley Community College has witnessed remarkable results from the First Year Experience program. It has grown from just over 50 sections in 2000 to over 170 courses serving more than 2,500 students in spring 2003 (J. Wright, personal communication, February 12, 2003). Cohort tracking of fall 2002-2003 groups indicates that students who had successfully completed COL-101 during their first semester earned higher cumulative grade point averages (GPAs) during their first and second semesters (GPA = 2.78 first semester, 2.62 cumulative) than students who did not complete or enroll in the course (GPA= 2.6 first semester, 2.57 cumulative for students who did not take the course, and 1.28 first semester, 1.25 cumulative for unsuccessful completers). In addition, data suggest that successful completers of COL-101 demonstrated a persistence rate of 75% across the year, while students who did not take the course or were unsuccessful were retained at 48% and 45% respectively (Manley, Taylor, & Wright, 2003).

CREATE AND OFFER MANY OPTIONS FOR LEARNING

O'Banion's (1997) third principle, which is to "create and offer as many options for learning as possible" (p. 47), requires institutions to rethink traditional forms for the delivery of educational opportunities to students. Renegotiating time, place, structure, staffing, support, and delivery methods requires colleges to step "out of the box" and consider alternatives that will reach students in an effective way. The Community College of Denver's (CCD) high school concurrent enrollment program offers an example of one way in which community colleges can address this principle.

The main campus of CCD, which opened in 1970, is in the heart of downtown Denver. It has four satellite campuses strategically located to meet the specific needs of local neighborhoods (Roueche, Ely, & Roueche, 2001). These branch campuses offer fast-track technical training and GED and core-level courses. In addition, CCD's Health Sciences Center houses health-care–related programs (nursing, dental hygiene, radiology technology, and veterinary technology, among others) (Community College of Denver Annual Report, 2003).

CCD reported a 2002-2003 enrollment of 13,529, with the ethnic breakdown consisting of 32% Latino/Hispanic, 16% African-American/Black, 2% Native American, 6% Asian/Pacific Islander, and 41% White students (Community College of Denver, 2003, p. 8). Forty-one percent of CCD's total student population is considered low-income, based on Pell grant recipients (Community College of Denver Annual Report, 2003).

Since 1998, high school concurrent enrollment options have been available for all Colorado high school students (Postsecondary Enrollment Options Act of 1998). Public high school students in the 11th and 12th grades may take up to six credit hours per semester at a Colorado college or university and be reimbursed through the local school district for tuition costs upon successful completion of the course; 12th-graders who have completed all graduation requirements for high school may take additional credits. A high school student could conceivably earn up to 24 credit hours toward a college degree by the time he/she graduates from high school. Students enrolled in private or charter high schools may also receive high school and college credit; however, tuition is not reimbursed through the school district (Postsecondary Enrollment Options Act of 1998). Students may not only take courses on any one of the college campuses but also may take advantage of many course offerings at their local high schools and in select community nonprofit agencies.

Though many institutions of higher education offer opportunities for extended learning through area high schools, CCD's model is distinctive in that it delivers a variety of options for high school students based on the unique needs of the community. Working with high school counselors and administrators, CCD identifies courses that fit within the high school culture. For example, courses in English as a Second Language are offered at a high school with a high percentage of non-native English-speaking students. College core courses are offered at traditional and dropout retrieval high schools to introduce college as an option to students who are not necessarily college-bound. And a Certified Nurses Aide preparatory program introduces an alternative career track to students in low-income neighborhoods who don't have an abundance of college options.

A model partnership that uses high school concurrent enrollment principles is the Career Education Center (CEC) High School. CEC, an alternative high school, focuses on preprofessional, career-oriented academic programs. Through high school concurrent enrollment, CCD offers on-site college-level courses in health, fire science, criminal justice, and computer information technology that complement and extend CEC offerings (Community College of Denver Recruitment Data, 2004). In 2003, CEC formalized its partnership with CCD by launching the CEC Middle College of Denver High School. The middle college offers students a seamless educational track from completion of a high school diploma toward matriculation into an associate's degree program at CCD. Case management of all students provides a comprehensive introduction to college through orientation programs and campus tours, enrollment and registration assistance, and transportation to and from the college campus for their courses.

A second early college opened in fall, 2004. Again in partnership with CCD, Southwest Early College (SEC) is an independent charter high school funded, in part, by the Middle College National Consortium. SEC will provide a traditional high school curriculum in the 9th and 10th grades and high school concurrent courses in the 11th and 12th grades. SEC is located on CCD's newest branch campus.

Successful coordination of CCD's high school concurrent enrollment program requires that instructional and student service divisions work collaboratively at many levels. Curriculum design and articulation agreements, negotiation of faculty contracts, classroom scheduling, enrolling and transcription of student records, and development of accurate data reporting mechanisms require that CCD envision high school concurrent enrollment as a program owned by the entire college, rather than one division or department.

Enrollment in the CCD high school concurrent enrollment program has grown from approximately 40 students in FY 2002 to 437 students taking 1,711 credit hours in FY 04 (Community College of Denver Recruitment Data, 2004). In spring 2004, 17 college courses were offered on-site at Denver area high schools (Community College of Denver Recruitment Data, 2004). Overall, CCD captures nearly 53% of all students in the Denver Public School district who take advantage of high school concurrent enrollment (C. Walters, personal communication, October 11, 2004). Spring 2003 grade analyses of high school concurrent enrollment students indicated that 84.29% passed their college courses with a grade of

"C" or better (Community College of Denver Recruitment Data, 2004). Moreover, high school students who have taken at least one college course prior to graduation were 50% more likely to matriculate as a regular degree- or certificate-seeking student at CCD (Community College of Denver Recruitment Data, 2004).

ASSIST LEARNERS IN FORMING AND PARTICIPATING IN COLLABORATIVE LEARNING ACTIVITIES

The fourth learning college principle developed by O'Banion focuses on the importance of assisting learners to form and participate in collaborative learning activities (O'Banion, 1997). Traditionally, these activities were offered through academic divisions. But with the increasing diversity of both the college classroom and the level of academic preparedness, institutions are seeking to develop a community of learners coordinated through student services divisions, recognizing and accepting these services as part of the academic pedagogy.

Information from research and interviews with staff and students involved in student services divisions at both 2-year and 4-year academic institutions makes it evident that several factors must be in place for an implementation to be successful. These include buy-in from the top down, budgetary support, a clearly defined program mission, consistent training and follow-up, and well-defined outcome measures.

A successful example is the Supplemental Instruction Program offered at the Community College of Baltimore County (CCBC) in Maryland. CCBC has three campuses and two major extension centers throughout suburban Baltimore County (Community College of Baltimore County, Institutional Profile, n.d.). Enrollment at CCBC is approximately 60,000 students. CCBC's institutional emphasis on student learning has earned it the distinction of being one of 12 Vanguard Learning Colleges in the United States and Canada. Its Supplemental Instruction (SI) program is an example of students helping students, with leadership, coordination, training, and support provided by college personnel, administrators, and faculty.

SI was developed by Deanna Martin in 1973 at the University of Missouri and is an academic assistance program that focuses on increasing student performance and retention (Burmesiter, 1996). Students learn the appropriate application of study strategies—e.g., note taking, graphic organization, questioning techniques, vocabulary acquisition, and test preparation—as they review content material.

SI leaders are also students, a key component in the success of the program. These student leaders function as model students rather than authority figures. They demonstrate proficiency in the content area as well as modeling the learning processes necessary for content mastery (*Overview of Supplemental Instruction*, n.d.).

SI sessions are designed to promote student interaction and mutual support. Such interaction leads to the formation of peer study groups and facilitates the mainstreaming of culturally diverse as well as disadvantaged students. SI has relied upon the power of group study for its success (*Overview of Supplemental Instruction*, n.d.).

The director of the Student Success Center attributes the success of the SI program to several components. One is following a clearly defined program with guidelines for ongoing training, participation, and follow-up support. SI student leaders take part in a 2-day training session before the beginning of the semester. They attend class each time it meets. Trained professional staff members who periodically attend the SI sessions provide supervision.

There is also a high level of faculty support, which strengthens the link between academics and services provided through student service divisions. Faculty members are involved in the selection of SI leaders, and the SI program is offered only in classes where the faculty member understands and supports SI.

Program evaluation is another important component. The SI program is evaluated by assessing outcome measures (such as final course grades, course withdrawal rates, dropout rates, and graduation rates). When possible, SI program studies should control for prior academic performance of students.

DEFINE THE ROLES OF LEARNING FACILITATORS BY THE NEEDS OF LEARNERS

O'Banion's fifth learning college principle states, "The learning college defines the roles of learning facilitators by the needs of learners" (1997, p. 57). The term "learning facilitator" describes all employees in the learning college. Implicit in this term is the notion that all employees are responsible in part for facilitating student learning. This includes employees previously considered inessential to the learning process, such as physical plant staff, information technology professionals, classified/ support staff, and student affairs professionals. This transformation of professional roles and respon- sibilities is implemented to meet the evolving needs of student learners and should be reflected in the creation of new jobs, job descriptions, hiring practices, and even delivery of services.

The Community College of Baltimore County's Online Academic Advising System is an excellent example of O'Banion's this principle in action. The system is a comprehensive model of cyber services developed in response to the needs of its learners. CCBC's Online Academic Advising System features frequently asked questions for credit and noncredit stu- dents and includes links to and information on academic programs and student support services (Community College of Baltimore County, 2004). It also features an "Ask an Advisor" interactive website in which a cyber adviser responds to inquiries (Hall & Zlotowitz, personal communication, July 8, 2004). This system serves as a one-stop shop for student inquiry in which practically any question regarding the learning experience at CCBC can be answered.

Several notable results have come out of the implementation of the Online Academic Advising System. One is the collaboration of student affairs with the Continuing Education Department to offer the Web-based system. This new service has improved services for distance- and extended-learning students, international learners, and any learner who is unable to or chooses not to access these services on campus. With its personalized advising sessions with the cyber adviser, this system also eliminates much of the red tape students encounter in the initial inquiry process. In the first two months of the system's launch, the cyber adviser counseled at least 50 students per week, a caseload comparable to that of a traditional adviser and indicative of learners' need for this service (H. Zlotowitz, personal communication, July 8, 2004).

Several factors led to the successful implementation of CCBC's Online Academic Advising System. First, the learning college fully supported the development of this system and allocated operational funds for it. Second, collaboration and buy-in of all stakeholders were important in developing this initiative. A third factor was the persistence of the Online Academic Advising Committee, despite the laborious nature of this project. The committee included representatives from advising and counseling, information technology, continuing education, distance and extended learning, and records and registration. It was led by student affairs administrators. The committee leadership identified three factors key to the successful implementation of this initiative: excellent administrative skills, effective advocacy, and technological expertise (P. Hall, personal communication, July 8, 2004).

DOCUMENT IMPROVED AND EXPANDED LEARNING

The final of O'Banion's (1997) six learning college principles indicates that the learning college gauges success when improved and expanded learning is documented for its learners. This principle asks two key questions: "What have students learned?" and "How do we know?"

Valencia Community College (VCC) in Orlando, Florida, is one example of an institution that has done an outstanding job of capturing the complete role of student services in extending student learning while documenting performance indicators such as retention rates and student satisfaction. VCC is a large community college that serves a two-county district with four campuses and several centers. LifeMap is Valencia's trademark developmental advising system, which links students to resources, information, and services (VCC, LifeMap, n.d.). The system outlines the roles of faculty and staff in developmental advising and serves as an overall learning companion to students. LifeMap epitomizes O'Banion's (1997) sixth learning college principle as it helps students identify goals, establish learning plans, and document completion of learning objectives and mastery of core competencies.

LifeMap breaks down the student experience into five progressive stages. Learning outcomes and performance indicators at each stage are aligned with programs and services that help students acquire skills and achieve learning. Various means of documentation are used at each stage. An example of student services' involvement in this multi-pronged process is briefly described below.

The "introduction to college" stage of LifeMap helps learners transition to the college. In this stage are over 24 programs and services to help to learners meet the five success indicators (VCC, LifeMap, n.d.). Two examples of the involvement of student affairs in this stage are Cyber Adviser and Cyber Career services. Cyber Adviser is educational planning software developed by VCC to help students create plans that meet graduation requirements and achieve their educational goals. These plans are an early step in the documentation of student learning. Cyber Career allows students to do self-assessments to explore self, majors, and careers. Members of the Career Center staff review responses with learners, and learners store this information in cyber portfolios.

CREATE AND NURTURE AN ORGANIZATIONAL CULTURE THAT IS OPEN AND RESPONSIVE TO CHANGE AND LEARNING

Harvey-Smith's (2003) seventh learning college principle is to create and nurture an organization that is both open and responsive to change and learning. It directs renewed attention and understanding to the heart of the institution—its people. It focuses attention on creating cultures of inclusion, support for all learners, and a desire to engage community members in order to actualize learning-centered principles and practices.

Establishing these cultures in student affairs divisions is an excellent way to demonstrate leadership in cultural transformation. The Community College of Baltimore County–Catonsville Campus Division of Learning and Student Development is establishing new benchmarks in this area.

The division focuses on creating supportive learning cultures for faculty, staff, and students. It is committed to measuring learning, integrating academic and social spheres, providing college-wide leadership, functioning beyond traditional roles, communicating and connecting, encouraging student leadership and comprehensive development, and creating an institutional environment that is open and responsive to change and learning.

New students are introduced to the learning culture through orientation, student development courses, and learning communities. The orientation includes a sample class experience. Information explaining the learning college experience and expectations is also provided in an orientation edition of the campus' *Learning First* newspaper.

The division recognized that orienting new students to the college is critical, and it applies the learning college principles to acclimate students to the new environment and to clarify their expectations. This approach has made the difference in student learning, retention, and success.

The main goal of the orientation program is to facilitate a new student's transition into the college environment. The orientation program acclimates students, provides them with a connection to college resources, and helps them to form connections within the college community. In addition, orientation provides a review of college services that include the facilities and environment, academic resources, and course selection and registration. The focus of orientation is on helping students understand what is expected of them and what they can expect from the institution.

New student orientations are conducted for both full- and part-time students. New full-time students are required to participate in a one-day orientation consisting of a sample class, where students meet with faculty to clarify expectations, discuss class syllabi, and participate in a college class. Students are also provided an opportunity to learn about the Achieving Academic Success-Student Development course, an opportunity to form relationships with peers through small group sessions, lunches with peers and college faculty and staff, an interactive tour of all available campus resources, a comprehensive advisement presentation, and small group advisement and registration.

After orientation, students are encouraged to register for the Achieving Academic Success-Student Development 101 course during their first semester. This course is also highly recommended to developmental studies students and those considered high-risk.

The course explains the significance of a college education as well as the ways that the college can partner with students to achieve their goals. It also provides an opportunity for students to discuss how they are responsible for their experience in college and ways that they can create a successful and satisfying college experience. The course is 15 weeks in length, although accelerated 6- and 7-week courses have been offered. Upon successful completion, students earn 3 credits.

Instructors include instructional faculty, counseling faculty, student services faculty and staff, continuing education administrators, and others. An all-day training session is conducted in the summer, and mentoring and internships for prospective teachers are offered. Instructors meet during the semester to share ideas, challenges, and successes. Research from anonymous evaluations has found that over 90% of the students who take the course say they would recommend it to a friend. Retention data show that between 87% and 91% of the students who pass the course in the fall with a "D" or better come back in the spring.

In addition to coordinating the orientation program, the student affairs division runs the learning community program. Two full-time faculty members compensated by overload or release time facilitate the effort.

Learning communities restructure the curriculum to link courses or material to foster what has been described as greater educational coherence for students (Cox, 1993). The learning communities model on the Catonsville campus seeks to link existing courses and restructure the curriculum through faculty and staff partnerships, so that students have increased opportunities for deeper understanding and integration of the material they are learning. Learning communities are available to all students and are highly recommended to entering students in an effort to build community and support for all learners.

CONCLUSION

The vision of student affairs divisions aligning practices, policies, and programs in support of learning college principles could not be more timely, as the role of student affairs shifts to the center of the discourse on learning in the academy. Student affairs divisions in learning organizations that adapt and align practices and systems to more effectively support improved and expanded learning will provide a comprehensive view of the learning experience and serve students in new ways.

Figure 1 provides examples of how specific student affairs practices can be aligned structurally, procedurally, and culturally in response to the seven learning college principles.

Figure 1: Sample Alignment of Practices with Learning College Principles in Student Affairs

Harvey-Smith (2003). Format adopted from Miles & Huberman (1994), Case Dynamics Matrix.

Core Principle	How to Address: Types of Resulting Change
1. Create substantive change in learner	Redesign programs to focus on outcomes Implement comprehensive retention system Establish partnerships with instructional teams and community partners to develop new ways to help students see, think, and do. Cultural, Structural, Procedural Changes
2. Engage learners as full partners	Create developmental advising model – with goal of self-sufficiency Increase dialogue and interactions through orientations and learning communities to ensure academic success and continuous engagement. Provide students with tools and opportunities for experimentation Cultural, Structural, Procedural Changes
3. Create and offer a variety of learning options	Expand presentations, student success courses, dual enrollment, precollege programs, distance-learning, weekend, and summer programs Expand cocurricular programs; expand options for high-risk students, learning camps. Rethink traditional forms of service delivery Cultural, Structural, Procedural Changes
4. Assist learners in forming and participating in collaborative learning activities	Offer student life cocurricular programming, learning communities, internships, service learning, varied course offerings, chat rooms Embed collaborative approach throughout programs and services Provide peer mentoring, tutoring, supplemental instruction Cultural, Structural, Procedural Changes
5. Define roles in response to needs of learners	Reexamine role, which may culminate in redesign; transitioning from independent role to integrated role; consider online advising efforts, and other independent learning experiences Recognize all have role in facilitating learning Cultural, Structural, Procedural Changes
6. Document improved and expanded learning	Build culture of evidence through cyber portfolios, goal team reports, internal and external assessments, placement, success, retention rates Document student learning throughout engagement with services and programs, link to core competencies Cultural, Structural, Procedural Changes
7. Create and nurture an organizational culture that is open and responsive to change and learning	Do culture audit; leaders model espoused behaviors; authentic communication and genuine collaboration take place; focus on fostering relationships; encourage and reward risk taking; all community members are learners, opportunities for input are ongoing, Past contributions are acknowledged and reflected upon. Systems are open and diverse; there are high levels of trust and willingness to innovate Cultural, Structural, Procedural Changes

By determining how each of the learning college principles can be actualized from the worldview of student affairs, cultural, procedural, and structural changes may be realized. The 21st-century learning college is made better and the learning college vision is made real by strong, engaged student affairs divisions whose policies, practices, and programs are aligned to improve learners and the cultures that serve and nurture them.

REFERENCES

Blue Chip Leadership Program at University of Arizona. (n.d.). Retrieved July 5, 2004, from http://www.union.arizona.edu/csil/bluechip/preview.php

Burmesiter, S. (1996). Supplemental Instruction: An interview with Deanna Martin. *Journal of Developmental Education, 20*(1), 22-24, 26.

Community College of Baltimore County Institutional Profile (n.d.). Retrieved July 8, 2004, from http://ccbcmd.edu/vanguard/profile.html

Community College of Baltimore County. (2004). Online Academic Advising Center online advising. Retrieved July 8, 2004, from http://www.ccbcmd.edu/advisement/online

Community College of Denver. (2003). *Community College of Denver Annual Report.* Denver, CO: Author.

Community College of Denver. (2004). CCD Recruitment Data. Unpublished internal document.

Cox, B. (Ed.). (1993). *Learning communities in teacher education programs: Four success stories.* (Report No. RC-019-701). Claremont, CA: Tomas Rivera Center. (ERIC Document Reproduction Service No. ED 372 888)

Dungy, G., & Clements, E. (Eds.). (2003). *Bridges to student success: 2003 exemplary programs.* Champaign, IL: National Council on Student Development (NCSD) National Office.

Harvey-Smith, A. B. (2003). *The adoption of the learning paradigm in student affairs divisions in Vanguard community colleges.* Unpublished doctoral dissertation, University of Maryland, College Park.

Jennings, S., McCabe, M., & Strickland, C. (2004). The Student Medallion Leadership Institute: Inspiring holistic learning and leadership. *Leadership Abstracts, 17*(4). Retrieved July 6, 2004, from http://www.league.org/publication/abstracts/leadership/labs0404.htm

Manley, C., Taylor, D., and Wright, J. (2003, October). *First Year Experience at Moraine Valley Community College.* Presentation at National Council on Student Development conference, St. Louis, MO.

Miles, M., & Huberman, A. (1984). *People, policies, and practice: Examining the chain of school improvement: Vol. IV. Innovation up close: A field study in twelve school settings—a study of dissemination efforts supporting school improvement.* Andover, MA: Network of Innovative Schools, Inc.

Moraine Valley Community College Enrollment and Student Characteristics. (n.d.). Retrieved June 28, 2004, from http://www.morainevalley.edu/InstResearch/enrollment/enrollme.htm

National Center for Educational Statistics. (n.d.). Retrieved July 1, 2004, from http://nces.ed.gov/globallocator

O'Banion, T. (1997). *A learning college for the 21ˢᵗ century.* Phoenix, AZ: Oryx Press.

Overview of Supplemental Instruction. (n.d.). Retrieved July 1, 2004, from http://www.umkc.edu/cad/si.htm

Pima Community College Quick Facts. (n.d.). Retrieved July 2, 2004, from http://www.pima.edu/dept/about/facts.htm

Pima Community College Student Profile. (n.d.). Retrieved July 2, 2004, from http://www.pima.edu/dept/about/studprof

Postsecondary Enrollment Options Act, Colo. Rev. Stat. §§22-101-111 (1998).

Roueche, J., Ely, E., & Rouche, S. (2001). *In pursuit of excellence: The Community College of Denver.* Washington, DC: Community College Press.

Valencia Community College LifeMap. (n.d.). LifeMap. Retrieved July 9, 2004, from http://valenciacc.edu/LIFEMAP/MORE_LIFEMAP.ASP

CHAPTER 8

Aligning Student Affairs in a Learning-Centered College

Sanford C. Shugart and Joyce Romano

*"The real discovery consists not in finding new lands,
but in seeing with new eyes."*

—MARCEL PROUST

INTRODUCTION

A wise friend who was both a brilliant leader (a former governor of North Carolina) and a dairy farmer once said he loved farming except for one thing: "Dang cows won't stay milked!" In much the same way, the work of student affairs is driven by a demand for continuous transactional services—recruiting, assessing, advising, orienting, registering—that seems to flow more than ebb and create such a focus on operational success that strategic issues are rarely dealt with at all. Often, student affairs divisions know they are consumed, to borrow a phrase, with "doing things right, rather than doing the right things."

The learning college paradigm challenges this operational habit. When a college defines its work in terms of the results for learners, we are compelled to ask not only if our operating systems are working for our immediate goals (efficient and effective enrollment services, best use of financial aid, robust enrollment growth, every student properly placed) but also that success in these goals leads to success in the learning goals. These immediate goals determine much of our enrollment and therefore our revenue. Failure in these will surely spell failure for our mission. Success in these, however, does not necessarily mean success as a learning college.

One of the serious challenges to student affairs leaders in colleges committed to reengineering themselves to get better learning results, then, is how to continue to deliver the essential operational results while redesigning and redeploying major systems to get better learning results. This is somewhat akin to renovating the kitchen while preparing a state banquet for 5,000 guests.

LEARNING COLLEGE SYSTEMS

A learning-centered student affairs organization applies "learning" as its central design principle (Barr & Tagg, 1995). This means that the organization is designed so that all the systems combine to create the optimal conditions for student learning. Student affairs, like other components of the college, fulfills this role by asking at each point of systems design, "How does this improve or enhance learning?" and "How do we know?" (O'Banion, 1997)

Let's say again for emphasis, this is systems work. Other parts of the college may get away with working in silos, accommodating idiosyncratic approaches to work, even encouraging a sort of rugged individualism among faculty. In student affairs, however, the nature of the work requires systemic solutions.

Student affairs has an advantage, in that systems thinking, though typically operational in scope, has been a part of the culture for many years. One simply can't integrate services any other way. Seeing how changes in one part of the process may have consequences for others is a mature perspective in student affairs. The question, then, is how to take this systems perspective and translate it into strategic thinking and redesign to get better learning results with students, rather than merely tweaking the systems for better operational results.

This kind of work requires powerful, galvanizing, big ideas. Such ideas incorporate all the complexity of the systems and the simplicity and focus necessary to get results. These big ideas are vitally important. In his marvelous book, *Good to Great* (2001), Jim Collins calls them the "hedgehogs" in companies that have transformed themselves into consistently great performers. These are the insights into the architecture of our work around which we can organize our efforts to improve. They are whole new ways of looking at the work. Over the past 10 years at Valencia Community College, these big ideas have been essential to the work that has transformed our student affairs model of work.

Following a bit of background on Valencia, we will summarize our big ideas and show how they are manifested in the systems.

VALENCIA COMMUNITY COLLEGE

Founded in 1969 in Orlando, Florida, Valencia Community College serves some 50,000 credit students per year (unduplicated head count), with about two thirds pursuing transfer programs and one third technical degrees and certificates. It is a multi-campus college (Valencia, 2004a). Valencia began earnest dialogue about the learning college paradigm in the early 1990s, using grants and working with partners such as the Kellogg Foundation and ACE. Thoughtful review of the Student Affairs Division revealed fragmentation of services across campuses and departments, some silos of departments and operations that needed integration, and a lack of tools and staff to meet student learner needs beyond optimizing enrollment. Members of the staff revealed dissatisfaction with the student success rates, a deep commitment to student success, and a willingness to reengineer their work to get better results.

Early in this process, the division was centralized from relatively independent campus departments of student services to a college-wide division. Campus deans of students, who had previously reported directly to campus provosts, instead began reporting directly to a college vice president for educational programs (student services). They remained a part of the campus leadership team but had a "dotted line" to the campus leaders and a "solid line" to the vice president. This improved the college's ability to introduce systemic reform to the division.

Also early on, the college was challenged with the question, "What is your underlying theory or model of student services?" This question revealed that the college had been focused on perfecting its operations and needed to revisit its mission and systems. The college began to look for a unifying conceptual framework, grounded in the literature and research of student development, human learning and motivation, and higher education. After much discussion, a model of student advising that blended the ideas expressed in the work of Frost (1991), O'Banion (1994), Gordon and Sears (1997), and Tinto (1993) was developed. The college learned that the model must be described from the student perspective and include the ideal progression of student learning and development.

This model is important for several reasons. It demystifies the college experience for students so they can learn how to optimize their own learning. It provides an organizational theme around which faculty and staff can contribute to student success. Finally, it provides a core model for designing interventions and evaluating their success, troubleshooting solutions, and interpreting the assessments of impact on students. The model supplies the language of reform and the basis for evaluation.

Having established a theory of student engagement and a model of student service, the college began to redesign its services. In this process, five "big ideas" have emerged as design principles. Each is briefly described below.

CONDITIONS OF LEARNING

Historically, effective student services systems have been designed to "deliver the right student to the right class at the right time, ready to learn." This is the best of the operational definitions we have found for a traditional approach to student services, and it still has much validity. To this requirement, however, we have to add a responsibility. Learning colleges seek to improve student learning by creating the optimal conditions for each student's learning, and this is not just a concern for academic affairs. Defining the conditions of learning—the alterable variables in the learning equation—and seeking to optimize them at every opportunity is the focus of system redesign in student affairs. The most important of these variables are time, engagement, assessment, challenge, and heart (we use the acronym T.E.A.C.H. to provide a simple reference point for all staff) (Astin, 1993; Gardiner, 1993; McKeachie, 2002; Tinto, 1997). These are easily recognized as variables in the classroom. They also have important implications for student affairs. In a nutshell, then, the whole college seeks to make systemic changes that lead to improvements in

1. Time on task, both in and out of the classroom
2. Engagement of students with their academic work, one another, their professors, and the college staff
3. Accurate and timely individualized assessment of learning results, first for the learner, then for the teacher, and finally for the institution
4. Challenge, or expectations for performance that communicate to the students our confidence in their capacity to learn all we have to teach and clearly assign the responsibility (while providing the tools) to students for the lion's share of the learning enterprise
5. Heart, or the belief that all students can learn under the right conditions in every discipline, curriculum, and course.

With these touchstones for design, one can ask many powerful questions, such as: How does our orientation program prepare students to invest the time to succeed? Have we created a campus culture and climate that is engaging for all students, or are some feeling less welcomed? Does our system of assessment and placement assure accurate placement of every student? Is it viewed as a positive preparatory step or a punitive, remedial one? Does our assessment system provide the learner and the teacher with helpful insights into the learning strengths and preferences of each learner? Does our staff exhibit a passion for the learning of our students, or have we so exhausted them that students have become to them a problem to be solved rather than people with potential to be developed?

CONNECTION AND DIRECTION

Learning is not a passive activity. It engages the learner and requires that the college create an engaging climate. The literature of student persistence and success is quite clear on the importance of making an early connection (Tinto, 1997; Stahl, Simpson, & Hayes, 1992). These connections are important in every dimension: student to curriculum, student to staff, student to student, and student to faculty. In our large and often impersonal bureaucracies, many students float through without connection and are at high risk of attrition. Our evidence suggests that no time is more vital for this connection than the very first experiences of college. Certainly, academic success is highly correlated to persistence. So is a positive experience in the first interactions on campus with, typically, student affairs staff. These interactions must simplify the bewilderment many students experience upon entering college, clarify what their next step will be, and give them the tools to succeed there, at the front door of the college. Front-line staff members play a critical role here; we call them "directors of first impressions." By this, we don't just mean the students' impressions of the college but also their impressions of themselves. These impressions should assure the students that no matter how overwhelming this may all seem, they are perfectly capable of succeeding here.

It isn't enough, though, that students make a connection to the college. As early as possible, they must also develop a clear sense of direction. Students bring three important "directional" questions to student affairs:

1. What do I do next? Here we give the kind of advice that we are best at, sorting out the complexities of our processes, our regulations, our deadlines, our software, our bureaucracy. The information is valuable but not particularly empowering.

2. What do I do here? This involves decisions about program, course sequence, prerequisites, and major that constitute for most students a rough academic plan. Some colleges do an admirable job with this work. Most haven't a clue. The typical community college requires students to file a plan to graduate the semester they graduate. It is called an "application for a degree." Yet having a plan early

in one's career has a demonstrably positive impact on one's chances of success (Tinto, 1993). A learning college will make it possible for all students to have a meaningful plan to graduate on file as early as possible in their academic career, perhaps by the 15th credit hour.

3. What do (or will) I do? This is a matter of serious career and life discernment. Many colleges offer services in this area, but they are rarely accessed by more than a small percentage of the students. Yet having clarity on this matter is the foundation for good answers to the first two questions.

Connection and direction have proven to be very powerful ideas at Valencia. When students meet three criteria of connection and direction, their likelihood of graduating is extremely high: If they complete any required remediation, attempt at least 15 hours of college credit work, and declare a major, their graduation rates approach 90%. Still, at Valencia the most powerful predictor of successful completion of a program is academic performance in the first semester.

START RIGHT

One of the richest sources of data on student performance is transcripts. Transcript analysis offers us a view of the college as the students experience us, not as we experience them. One helpful approach to these data is to assess the accumulated credit hours of all enrolled students. If there were no attrition and no failure, one would expect an almost equal number of students with 15 hours as with 30, or even 60 hours. Indeed, this is the pattern one finds at Ivy League colleges. In a typical community college, however, one finds that nearly 80% of the students have accumulated 15 or fewer semester hours. This is the nut of the educational challenge faced by the American community college. We continue to enroll large numbers of students in order to produce relatively few graduates. The fact is, if students survive the early experiences of a community college, they tend to succeed at a rather high level. However, very few survive these early experiences. Despite many years of effort, most community colleges still churn large numbers of students in and out of the front door.

This means that systemic improvements and investments at the 30th or 40th hour of the curriculum will have only minor impact on graduation, placement, and transfer. Even modest improvements early in the process could produce far-reaching effects. Valencia and other colleges on the learning paradigm journey, therefore, are concentrating much of their effort on the first experiences of the college. We call this principle "start right."

COLLABORATION

We recently went through an inclusive process to hire a chief student affairs officer. Throughout the process, the most frequently asked question was, "How will you collaborate with academic affairs in your work?" The recently hired chief academic officer admitted she was never asked in her extensive interviews how she would collaborate with student affairs.

This scenario might be taken to mean that old biases about the relative roles of academic and student affairs persist. It might also mean that student affairs has dealt itself into the learning college journey powerfully enough to be considered a player with which to be reckoned. We believe the latter is the case. Redesigning the model of student services has created such pervasive change that it can't be ignored in the classrooms and faculty lounges. Since its purpose is to alter the conditions of learning, the faculty now has a very real stake in the work. The student learning experience is continuous and does not divide itself along the college organizational boundaries. This movement creates the necessity for student affairs to partner more effectively with academic administrators, the faculty, administrative services, technology support, institutional research, and institutional advancement.

STUDENT AFFAIRS CURRICULUM

The traditional college curriculum, so famously fragmented by distributed requirements and disciplinary atomization, needs to be more carefully constructed so students experience it as an academic program and not just a collection of courses. An alternate view considers the content of student affairs as a curriculum and the processes as a pedagogy (Harvey-Smith, 2003). This creates the possibility of meta-cognitive outcomes, or core curricular outcomes that are touched by every learning experience. At Valencia, these have been defined by the faculty to be: Think, Value, Communicate, and Act. In every discipline, faculty teams are working to define how these outcomes are learned and assessed. But these outcomes ought to be designed into the student affairs "curriculum" as well. Since the learning college seeks to make active, and eventually independent, partners in learning out of the students, our processes should also have clearly articulated outcomes. What is it we want students to learn as they progress through the systems of student affairs? Surely we would say competence in planning, scheduling, making critically informed choices about one's future, understanding one's own learning styles and strengths, and employing this knowledge for one's learning. The point is that in a learning college, student affairs will define these outcomes and assess them.

A part of this big idea at Valencia is the notion of "Big A to the Big S." Shown in Figure 1, it is intended to convey to the student (the "S") and the college (all faculty and staff denoted as "A" – "Advisers") that we expect the student to play a modest role as a partner in managing his learning early in his career; as he progresses, he is expected to become increasingly self-sufficient and the college's role should diminish. As the student approaches graduation and transfer, he should be competent to manage the challenges of the next stage of his learning journey and also to have learned the process so he can repeat it as needed throughout his life. The student services curriculum should be designed to accomplish this transition.

Figure 1

A	As	AS	aS	S

SUMMARY OF THE BIG IDEAS

These five "big ideas"—creating the conditions for learning, assuring that our students experience connection and direction, assuring that our students start right, collaborating to build systems that work at the scale of the whole college, and being intentional about the curriculum of student affairs—have provided the intellectual leverage to develop and sustain long-term reform in student affairs based on the learning college paradigm. It is important to emphasize long term. The changes in the delivery model of student affairs at Valencia have been under way for nearly a decade, and the work still isn't complete. The extended time required for this kind of reform is one reason the big ideas are essential. When the project of the day bogs down or when staff members begin to ask themselves why they are stretching themselves for the next leg of the work, the big ideas lift them up out of the "weeds" of implementation and return them to the view from 10,000 feet. From this vantage point, they can both mark progress toward larger goals and map the course ahead.

THE SYSTEMS TRILOGY

Our big ideas have led Valencia to create three systems to provide operational performance and create a learning-centered student affairs environment for students. These three systems are LifeMap, Atlas, and the Learning-Centered Student Services Delivery Model. They are described below roughly in the order in which they were developed.

LifeMap

LifeMap is Valencia's developmental advising model. It is a system of responsibility shared by students, faculty, and staff that promotes social and academic integration, education and career planning, and the acquisition of study and life skills. Developmental advising assists students in the exploration, clarification, communication, and implementation of realistic choices, based upon awareness of their learning styles, abilities, interests, and values.

LifeMap recognizes that students typically enter college with vague notions of their goals and minimal understanding of how to negotiate a college environment. With the goal of student self-sufficiency, LifeMap interventions provide more support to students in the beginning of their college experience and then move them toward becoming more self-directed.

LifeMap is predominately about student goal-setting and planning. It includes creating a norm that says a student should have life, career, and educational goals; setting up a system to establish and document those goals; helping to plan and implement goals; developing assessment processes to re-evaluate goals; and documenting the achievement of goals. LifeMap describes for students "what they should do when" to achieve their career and educational goals through a five-stage model. Each stage includes an outcome, performance indicators, and guiding principles that tie to the literature on best practices. A time frame is specified in terms of academic progression.

The five stages are:

- Postsecondary Transition (middle and high school to college decision)
- Introduction to College (0-15 credit hours)
- Progression to Degree (16-44 credit hours)
- Graduation Transition (45-60 credit hours)

The details on each stage can be found at http://valenciacc.edu/lifemap/stages.

Once the model was developed, it became clear that change in student success would not occur until the LifeMap model was implemented through a system that supported it. The implementation process has included:

> **Gap Analysis.** With the LifeMap model as the ideal, we mapped the programs and services already in place to the LifeMap stages, refocused interventions where needed, and developed new interventions. With LifeMap as the foundation of the curriculum in student affairs, we have considered the learning outcomes, instructional strategies, and assessment methods for our programs. This has included integrating LifeMap into our new student orientation program, student success course, student services workshops, and individual advising sessions.

> **Faculty and Staff Development.** Faculty and deans have come to understand LifeMap as a means to tap into student motivation through understanding student goals and their connection to classroom learning experiences. Faculty development programs have provided opportunity to learn about and design instructional strategies that integrate LifeMap. Indeed, this is one of the competencies for new faculty who participate in the Teaching and Learning Academy. As the foundation for student affairs, LifeMap is integrated into all staff development programs, department meetings, and staff performance evaluations. Collaboration between student affairs and academic affairs has been a key to this work as we develop a system that reinforces for students the importance of goal setting and planning.

> **Marketing.** The brand name of "LifeMap" with the tag line "Life's a trip. You'll need directions." was developed to

explain developmental advising to students and motivate them to participate. Large banners on campus; posters in the hallways; collateral materials such as t-shirts, mouse pads, and other printed items; the redesign of college publications such as the student handbook; and the creation of new publications all contribute to integrating LifeMap into the culture of the college. The main call to action of the marketing campaign has been to urge students to have a plan (direction) and to point them to campus resources (connection).

Student Information System. LifeMap required a Web-based system that provided online tools for students to develop career and educational plans and to communicate easily with faculty and staff. Over time, we developed our online portal, Atlas.

Atlas

Atlas is a Web-based portal system that integrates numerous applications. Atlas connects students, faculty, and staff and encourages students to set direction for their learning, career, and educational goals early in their Valencia experience and to document their goal achievement.

Atlas was designed by an implementation team that included faculty, academic administration, admissions, financial aid, business office, advising, institutional research, continuing education, and information technology. An Academic Issues Task Force of faculty and academic deans recommended ways in which Atlas could support our learning-centered focus. The Faculty Association made recommendations on the implementation of features that served faculty. The Atlas Improvement Team continues as a representative group that guides ongoing development of Atlas.

Features that support connection and engagement are e-mail to all students, faculty, and staff; a home page for every course at Valencia that includes e-mail lists of the class, online syllabus, and other relevant links; a chat room; a message board; and Atlas groups that any person in the community can join or establish. The group categories were designed to support our learning goals. They include LifeMap: Students (groups created for each LifeMap stage), Career Interests, Majors, and Learning-Centered College. Each group has an e-mail list, links to information relevant to the group, a chat room, and a message board.

Atlas also includes a My LifeMap tab that contains four online planning tools as well as information about LifeMap, its stages, and the programs that support it. Students can use this information to assess their progress and connect with college resources. The tools—My Career Planner, My Education Plan, My Portfolio, and My Job Prospects—help students to do online career assessments and self-assessments; collect information on careers, majors, and transfer colleges of interest; evaluate gathered information via a summary; develop a list of career and educational goals based on this evaluation; develop plans for reaching these goals with deadlines; implement those plans; and track goal achievement. Faculty and advisers can review these plans with students and provide feedback. Students can review and edit their plans.

Atlas provides dynamic, time-relevant information and links to college services that guide students. An additional Atlas curriculum tool for student affairs is a messages feature, which sends "just in time" information to students. Messages either post on the Atlas home page or are e-mailed. Atlas also provides each student with information such as academic record, grades, degree audit, financial aid status, and student accounts. When registering, students can consult their My Education Plan to see the courses in which they should enroll, search for those classes and complete registration, make payments, and order books through Atlas.

To support our "start right" focus, we introduce Atlas to all new students in the orientation program, focusing on the My LifeMap tools and the academic services features. Online tutorials walk students through, and each campus has an Atlas Access lab with staff to assist students in learning the full functioning of the system. In the Student Success class in which all new students are encouraged to enroll, the curriculum includes time in the

Atlas Access lab to learn to use My Career Planner and My Education Plan. Students who complete the course (currently about one third of all entering students) create an education plan.

Learning-Centered Student Services Delivery Model

Student affairs is responsible for the processes of application, financial aid award and disbursement, assessment and placement, new student orientation, and advising and works closely with the business office on student accounts and fee payment. We know that these administrative processes are often frustrating to students and often create a negative early experience. In studying the literature on process engineering (Hammer & Champy, 1993; Hammer & Stanton, 1995; Beede & Burnett, 1999), we concluded that a major problem in the traditional delivery model is that students get information about what is really an end-to-end process (initial interest to seat in classes) in disjointed segments due to the traditional silos in which student services is delivered.

As a result, we redesigned our delivery model (see Figure 2) so that students learn the entire process in one physical location with the assistance of cross-trained staff members who focus on the learning process as opposed to just giving segmented answers. In fact, during the implementation of this model, we admonished staff not to answer students' first question, as it is often not the real question that students have. A conversation might go:

Student: "Can you tell me how I can get a transcript?"

Student Services Specialist: "Yes, but tell me what you want to accomplish so I can help you learn the entire process."

The conversation that follows may include discussion of degree and graduation requirements, possible administrative holds on the student's academic records, transfer planning, and referral to placement services.

Figure 2: Valencia Community College Learning-Centered Student Services Delivery Model

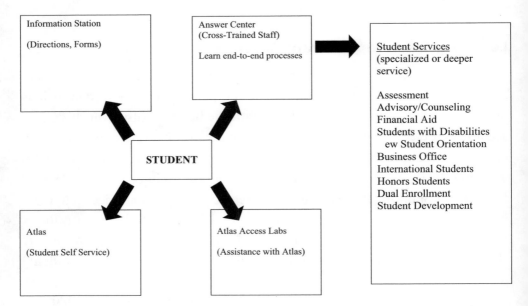

Our model was developed with the idea that 80% of student questions can be answered via Atlas. We support learning to use Atlas through para-professional staff available in the Atlas Access labs on campus, students' access to personal information through Atlas and the My LifeMap planning tools, and student engagement with professional staff in the Answer Center. Student services specialists in the Answer Center are cross-trained to help students learn the processes of admissions (application and residency), financial aid (application deadlines and materials, award and disbursement, and deadlines), transcripts (high school, college, advanced placement, College-Level Examination Program) and graduation (application, require-ments, commencement, deadlines). Specialists also make referrals to other student services staff if necessary. So they can focus on working with each student individually, the specialists do not have the responsibility of answering incoming telephone calls. Instead, telephone calls and e-mails are handled by the Enrollment Services Call Center, whose staff is also cross-trained to answer end-to-end process questions.

In the area now called Student Services, students meet with specialists in financial aid, counseling, advising, or specialized programs (e.g., honors, international students, dual enrollment). Managers in student services also have responsibility for programs such as new student orientation. These staff members are colocated so that students can go to one place for a number of specialized services. Still, some specialized services require their own location, such as services to students with disabilities, assessments, and the career services centers.

Another important piece of the redesign model was to separate the staff whose primary job is working directly with students and the staff whose primary job is processing and verifying information. For example, in traditional delivery models, the admissions staff members who enter large stacks of applications are also expected to assist students at the counter. Under these conditions, it is only human to feel that students are an interruption to one's work of "getting those applications done." We have created District Offices for admissions, financial aid, and graduation in which staff are responsible for the back office processing of student information, transcripts, applications, federal eligibility data, and so on, and are not expected to interrupt their work to answer telephones or serve students.

Physical space on the campuses has been redesigned to fit the new model with an improvement in efficiency and closer working relationships that benefit students. For example, the counselors and financial aid specialists are now in the same office suite; this has resulted in sharing of information and better understanding of how each other's processes affect students. New signage invites students to the Answer Center and other areas in a much more visible way. "Information Stations" in the lobby of each student services building also provide directional information, written materials, forms, and personal assistance by students trained as paraprofessionals.

Summary

The trilogy of LifeMap, Atlas, and Learning-Centered Student Services Delivery Model work together with the college's learning outcomes (Think, Value, Communicate, and Act [TVCA]) to form the content and the methodology for student affairs. LifeMap and TVCA form the content of "what" we are seeking to achieve with students, and Atlas and the Learning-Centered Student Services Delivery Model are the "how" we work with students to achieve those learning outcomes.

The assessment of the model has focused on traditional measures of student success—persistence, course completion, graduation. Results have improved in all measures, but, of course, Valencia's learning-centered college journey has included many more strategies than have been described here. With that as a caveat, some of the results we have seen are:

- Fall term to spring term persistence rate for first-time-in-college students was 79% in 2003-04, up from 65% in 1995-96 (Valencia, 2004a).

- The term-to-term persistence rate of new students who enroll in required developmental courses and take the Student Success course is 89%, compared with 56% for students who drop their developmental courses and do not take Student Success (Valencia, 2004a).

- Average number of credit hours completed increased to 8.7 in fall 2003 from 7.9 in fall 1994 (Valencia, 2004a).

- Valencia ranks No. 2 in the United States in the number of associate degrees awarded and No. 4 in associate degrees awarded to Hispanic students. In both cases, we are nowhere near the largest of colleges in terms of enrollment. The number of graduates is growing at more than twice the rate of enrollment growth (Community College Week, June 21, 2004).

- Over 12,000 students have saved a plan in My Education Plan, over 5,600 students have saved a career assessment in My Career Planner, and over 3,400 students have saved an entry in My Portfolio (Valencia, 2004b). While these are process rather than outcome measures, they are evidence of students' acceptance of LifeMap and its focus on planning.

CONCLUSION

Creating alignment in any large organization is a tremendous leadership challenge. Doing so in a division like student affairs with such unremitting operational demands is especially difficult. The journey toward a more learning-centered college is nearly a decade old at Valencia Community College, yet we are still in the formative stages of this transformation. Still, student affairs is in a leadership role in this transformation largely because the change is driven by five "big ideas."

The real work of transformation is in translating these ideas into systems of work. Though it is still early in their full implementation, the college is already beginning to see results that suggest more engagement, retention, and completion.

REFERENCES

Astin, A. (1993). *What matters in college.* San Francisco: Jossey-Bass.

Beede, M., and Burnett, D. (1999). *Planning for student services: Best practices for the 21ˢᵗ century.* Ann Arbor, MI: Society for College and University Planning.

Barr, R. B., and Tagg, J. (1995, November/December). A new paradigm for undergraduate education. *Change, 27*(6).

Collins, J. (2001). *Good to Great: Why some companies make the leap...and others don't.* New York: HarperCollins.

Frost, S. (1991). *Academic advising for student success.* Washington, DC: ASHE-ERIC.

Gardiner, L. F. (1993). Redesigning higher education: Producing dramatic gains in student learning. *ASHE-ERIC Higher Education Report, 23*(7). Washington, DC: The George Washington University, Graduate School of Education and Human Development.

Gordon, V., and Sears, S. (1997). *Academic alternatives: exploration and decision-making.* Upper Saddle River, NJ: Gorsuch Scarisbrick.

Hammer, M., and Champy, J. (1993). *Reengineering the corporation.* New York: Harper Business.

Hammer, M., and Stanton, S. (1995). *The reengineering revolution: A handbook.* New York: Harper Business.

Harvey-Smith, A. B. (2003). *The adoption of the learning paradigm in student affairs divisions in Vanguard community colleges.* Unpublished doctoral dissertation, University of Maryland, College Park.

McKeachie, J. (2002). *Teaching tips: Strategies, research, and theory for college and university professors.* Boston: Houghton Mifflin.

O'Banion, T. (1997). *A learning college for the 21ˢᵗ century.* Washington, DC: Oryx Press.

O'Banion, T. (1994). An academic advising model. *NACADA Journal, 14*(2), 10-16.

Stahl, N., Simpson, M., & Hayes, C. (1992). Ten recommendations from research for teaching high-risk students. *Journal of Developmental Education, 16*(1), 2-10.

Tinto, V. (1997). Classrooms as communities: Exploring the educational character of student persistence. *Journal of Higher Education, 68*(6), 599-623.

Tinto, V. (1993). *Leaving college: Rethinking the causes and cures of student attrition* (2ⁿᵈ ed.). Chicago: University of Chicago.

Valencia Community College (2004a). Fast Facts and Statistics, 2003/2004, published to the Web by Valencia Community College Department of Institutional Research. http://valenciacc.edu/aboutus/whoweare/fastfacts.asp

Valencia Community College (2004b). Unpublished report from Institutional Research, Valencia Community College, Orlando, FL.

CHAPTER 9

A Framework for Transforming and Sustaining Learning-Centered Student Affairs Divisions

Jack Becherer and Alicia B. Harvey-Smith

"Treasure every moment, for they will never reoccur."

—Japanese faculty member comment at tea ceremony

INTRODUCTION

You've been attending your favorite student development conference. You've cherished the opportunity to renew and revive and have enjoyed listening to stimulating speakers and learning current best practices. You're returning home, cruising at 30,000 feet, both literally and figuratively. Alas, the flight lands, and you've come back to earth. Tomorrow you return to work, which seems like a far different place than you've been hearing about at the conference.

The real work experience for most student development professionals is far removed from the exemplary programs and best practices highlighted at annual conferences. For every college that makes a commitment to become learner-centered, there are dozens that have not considered this possibility. For every student development professional who wants to apply the principles of learning centeredness, there are many colleagues who cannot imagine having this option. Even so, learning-centered practices are clearly present in colleges that do not officially proclaim themselves as learning organizations. This chapter will address ways to apply the philosophy and principles of a learning-centered college at institutions that are not officially embracing these concepts and ways that student development professionals can advance learning-centered practices in their colleges.

In this chapter, the terms "educator" and "teacher" refer to both academic faculty and student affairs practitioners. The traditional distinction between the "academic" teacher and the "student affairs" practitioner positions student affairs as secondary contributors to student learning. Learning-centered college cultures are most likely to succeed, however, when mutual respect exists among all college employees, when all faculty members hold equal value, and when everyone at a college—including faculty, administrators, support personnel, and students—is seen as contributing essentially to the learning process.

To illustrate the challenges student affairs practitioners face, consider the cases of two hypothetical student development professionals.

Mario is a counselor at a small, rural, publicly funded college. State revenues are down, and budgets at his college have been drastically reduced. Mario shares the counseling responsibilities with one other counselor and two educational planners, one of whom is half time. Mario's counseling colleague becomes ill and won't be able to work for the remainder of the year. However, since she has a great deal of sick leave and the college will continue to pay her salary, there's no money to replace her position. Therefore, Mario faces the challenge of being the only counselor. With so many students needing support, Mario does not know what services to continue and which ones to put on hold.

Sara is the dean of student development at an urban community college. She's been working with her division's faculty and staff to make nontraditional and diverse students feel more connected to the campus and more involved in out-of-class activities. Many programs have been initiated to accomplish these goals, and clear progress is being made. A new president at Sara's college implements a reorganization, merging student development and academic affairs and reassigning the responsibilities of each dean. Sara continues to manage the student services functions in her area and assumes responsibility for the college's learning resources center. One of the academic deans is assigned responsibility for counseling, advising, college life, and student leadership, the primary areas involved in the programs to increase student connectiveness. While much of the reorganization make sense to Sara, she's disappointed about being removed from programming that she is deeply invested in and worries that these initiatives will falter because the team that planned them has been changed.

Both Mario and Sara struggle to see how they can create a learning-centered environment for their students. Their challenges are not unusual. Many community college professionals feel that issues out of their control restrict their ability to do their jobs and maximize student learning. For these professionals, the invigorating sessions at professional development meetings are far removed from the reality of their jobs. And yet some find a way to overcome external factors.

COMMITMENT TO A LEARNING-CENTERED PHILOSOPHY

Learning-centeredness is foremost a state of mind that places students first. Fortunately, most educators care deeply about student learning. It is the primary reason they choose teaching or student affairs practice as their vocation. Palmer summarized an educator's passion for students by saying, "I am a teacher at heart, and there are moments that I can hardly hold the joy. When my students and I discover uncharted territory to explore, when the pathways out of the thicket open up before us, when our experience is illumined by the lightning-life of the mind—then teaching is the finest work I know" (1998, p. 1). Daily, most faculty members and student affairs staff bring a passion for learning to their jobs.

And yet most of our colleges seem unable to capitalize on the commitment of great educators to systemically place learning first. O'Banion's (1997) metaphor of "trimming the branches of a dying tree" strikes at the hearts of well-intentioned educational administrators who want to transform their colleges yet struggle to make noticeable change.

Why don't the efforts of great teachers and counselors translate into an institutional commitment to learning? Shouldn't the whole of an educational enterprise be at least as great as the sum of faculty efforts? What can be done to keep good educators from retreating to the sanctity of their classrooms and offices rather than participating in a total college commitment to change its culture?

Before learning-centeredness becomes a series of behavioral practices that change a college climate, it must become a shared state of mind for faculty, staff members, administrators, and students. Breaks in the chain of commitment strongly affect the culture of the organization as a whole. Two examples will illustrate this principle.

Mark is a competent student who unintentionally intimidates his teachers. He's a big man with a loud voice who overwhelms those around him. He frequently challenges his teachers' logic and, when dissatisfied with a test grade, questions their objectivity. Mark's challenges convey an implicit aggressiveness, and some of his teachers are concerned for their safety. One professor, after a particularly difficult exchange with Mark, approaches his departmental colleagues, who, after sharing stories, contact their student development dean and ask that Mark be removed from all of his classes.

Maria is an immigrant from Mexico who attends community college to learn English, receive her GED, and take courses to meet her dream of becoming a registered nurse. Maria struggles with her science classes, challenged by learning English as a second language, but works very hard and most often receives grades of "C." After two years, she completes her nursing prerequisites and applies for admission to the program. Unfortunately, the college has twice as many qualified students as spaces in the program. Since a student's success in prerequisite courses is a factor in the selection process, it is highly unlikely that Maria will ever be accepted. Despondent, Maria meets with her counselor for help, having no idea how she will gain access to training that will lead to a well-paying job to support her family.

In the first example, Mark's lack of impulse control and social skills cause concern among the faculty. His behaviors are unintentional yet bothersome, and his teachers, well aware of incidents of classroom violence elsewhere, demand that the student development dean take quick action. The dean, after speaking to Mark, believes that Mark can modify his demeanor with counseling and that he won't be physically aggressive. In addition, the dean knows of a similar situation at another college where a student, prematurely removed from his classes, brought legal action against the college and won a hefty settlement. Mark's teachers are angered by the administration's seeming lack of support and organize their colleagues to protest what they see as indifference to faculty safety.

In the second situation, a diligent, hard-working student can't overcome the complexity of learning science in a second language. Maria questions the value of the years she spent preparing for an unattainable degree. From her viewpoint, the college's policies seem cold and unyielding—the antithesis of a college that hoisted a banner across its student center reading, "We Place Students First!" As a mother active in her children's education and as a leader in the Latino community, Maria shares her frustration about the college with many people. They in turn complain that the college isn't meeting the needs of major sectors of the community or serving diverse populations. The nursing faculty and administration, on the other hand, point to a thoughtfully designed study that validates their admissions criteria and documents the relationship between good grades in prerequisite courses and a student's ability to complete a nursing degree. From the nursing department's perspective, the policy that kept Maria out of nursing saves many students from attempting a program that they lack the ability to complete. Maria's counselor is caught in the middle, understanding Maria's diligence but equally aware of the nursing department's effort to reduce the dropout rate.

Mark and Maria's scenarios demonstrate that carefully designed plans to implement a system-wide learning-centered philosophy can be thrown off by routine activities and encounters. Students exhibiting bothersome behaviors are commonplace, as are faculty concerns about the extent of administrative support for their safety. It is equally common for minorities to expect that their learning needs will be considered when developing criteria for programs with selective admission. Student affairs professionals often must balance the perspectives of both students and instructional colleagues as they find ways to promote a learning-centered culture while considering the viewpoint of academic affairs. Their journey toward a learning-centered focus can be examined from three vantage points: commitment to a learning-centered philosophy, establishing a cohesive architecture, and adopting a servant perspective.

A LEARNING-CENTERED PHILOSOPHY

Educational experiences outside of the classroom are critical components of a student's learning experience. Institutions with this learning-centered perspective on student affairs are moving in the right direction and demonstrate not only a richer understanding of student development but also a fuller appreciation of students and their engagement with the college environment. Support for this view of student affairs can be found in significant student affairs literature (American College Personnel Association, 1994; National Association of Student Personnel Administrators, 1987; Study Group on the Condition of Excellence in American Higher Education, 1984).

Understanding student outcomes in student affairs services can help institutions become more learning-centered. Determining what learning is to occur as a result of engaging in orientation programs; in learning communities; and as a result of involvement in clubs, organizations, or the myriad of other out-of-class learning experiences will make student affairs divisions more responsive to the learning paradigm. One strategy is to develop clear outcomes for services and programs based on institutional core competencies.

Student development plays a critical role in creating substantive change in learners. Additionally, student affairs professionals often can develop connections with students as a result of ongoing interactions with students who may not easily adjust to an academic institution's norms. Some colleges may attempt to advance a learning-centered climate while not emphasizing the contributions of student affairs staff. Although success might be achieved, it is difficult to imagine a lasting transformation in an institution that doesn't acknowledge the need to integrate all aspects of the student learning experience.

Promoting the outcome of learning by documenting student academic achievement is key to the learning enterprise (O'Banion, 1997). Student affairs must rise to the same standards of accountability that exist in academic affairs. For example, student affairs practitioners can examine retention and success rates, out-of-class involvement in activities, the impact of tutoring, the value of orientation programs, and benefits of advising and counseling services. It is important to determine what learning is anticipated and the method for measuring it.

As institutional processes are reviewed and more learning-centered changes are planned, student affairs professionals should examine how changes are communicated and if community members would characterize the communication as authentic. Authentic communication is grounded in honesty and increases the likelihood that information is favorably received. A learning-centered president remarked, "If communication is done simply to sell an idea, it isn't authentic." This level of truth in communication is necessary to achieve transformation and to make proposed processes and changes understandable and more palatable to community members. Open dialogues, facilitated by student affairs staff, provide opportunities for the institution to engage, reflect, and lessen the complexity of change by breaking the information into manageable components, reducing secrecy, and increasing support.

As new ideas are diffused into the organization, resistance can be reduced by soliciting and incorporating broad-based involvement early during the process, as diverse perspectives are used to reframe student development practices. By using cross-functional teams, a college creates a receptive climate for transformation, reducing challenge and resistance. The teams should include students, as learning organizations are improved when student perspectives are incorporated.

ARCHITECTURE AND COHESIVENESS

Establishing institutional and divisional architecture that facilitates learning-centered climates may prove crucial to success. As the architecture and its cohesiveness are aligned, the structures and resources should be aligned in support of expanded learning. An appropriate alignment will generate a synergy that will increase collaboration, heighten response to change, reduce institutional boundaries, and ignite integrated systems that are responsive to change. This meets the preconditions of a learning-centered college and formulates the underlying architecture needed for organizational transformation. What follows are five architectural components that facilitate learning-centered transformation.

1. **View the institution as a system where faculty, staff, and students promote learning.** Viewing the institution as a continuous system where all faculty, staff, and students have an equal stake in promoting learning is the first step in creating a learning-centered culture. Partnerships that support expanded and connected learning culminate in a variety of new learning models, blur lines across units, develop new vehicles for engaging students, and value the strength each partner brings to responding to the diverse needs of learners.

2. **Emulate innovative practices and exemplary programs.** Studying institutions that have successfully made the learning-centered transition provides an invaluable learning opportunity. A literature review will identify conceptual models to guide the work and accelerate change.

3. **Incorporate students into learning-centered planning.** It is important to solicit feedback from students when planning change. Student collaboration in decision making that affects course delivery is consistent with the learning-centered belief that students can guide organizational decisions by clarifying their needs.

4. **Develop a comprehensive system of development and assessment.** Once decisions are made and principles to advance learning-centeredness are developed, it is essential to design a system to assess the impact of the new principles. Adequately investing in measuring the value of initiatives is pivotal to making lasting change. Student affairs can play a significant role in documenting student achievement, especially when learning outcome assessment involves cocurricular experiences.

5. **Integrate and institutionalize change.** Once change in student affairs is initiated, it must be integrated into the strategic and operational priorities of the college. The integration of innovation into an organization's planning system increases the sustainability of change. While many initiatives begin as special projects that are disconnected from other institutional priorities, once implemented and proven valuable, they must be incorporated into core institutional functions.

A SERVANT PERSPECTIVE

What role do faculty and student affairs practitioners play in fostering student learning? What influence do student development educators have as leaders? Robert Greenleaf, author of *Servant Leadership*, suggests that those who have the opportunity to lead or influence others view themselves first and foremost as servants. Greenleaf offers a test for servant leaders:

"Do those served grow as persons; do they, while being served, become healthier, wiser, freer, more autonomous, more likely themselves to be servants? And what is the effect on the least privileged in society; will they benefit, or, at least, not be further deprived?" (p. 13).

Greenleaf describes the elements of servant leadership as including:

1. A willingness to take initiative
2. The capacity to elicit trust
3. An inclination to accept followers as they are

4. An ability to pace oneself, to reorient when direction needs to be changed, and to withdraw when the pressure of leading becomes too great.

Each element speaks to an ideal learning-centered environment. When taking initiative, for instance, student development practitioners naturally assume responsibility to guide the learning process. Knowing what is expected, with clearly defined deadlines and standards, helps practitioners enhance student success.

Trust and confidence are key components of effective interaction between student development professionals and their students. Students' trust in their counselor, educational planner, or financial aid adviser, accompanied by confidence in the direction provided by these professionals, forms the foundation to move beyond a student-to-helper encounter and toward a fulfilling relationship.

Unqualified acceptance of students requires a tolerance for imperfection. Greenleaf says, "The typical person—immature, stumbling, inept, lazy—is capable of great dedication and heroism if wisely led. Many otherwise able people are disqualified to lead because they cannot work with and through the half-people who are all there are. The secret of institution building is to be able to weld a team of such people by lifting them up to grow taller than they would otherwise be" (*Servant Leadership*, p. 21).

Finally, the ability to pace oneself, to reorient, and, when necessary, to withdraw acknowledges that leaders often have more to do than they are capable of. In order to take care of themselves, they must sort out the most from the least important and neglect some areas to devote adequate attention to others.

While each element of servant leadership speaks to the skills of a student development educator working to create a learning-centered environment, the capacity to elicit trust and the inclination to accept students as imperfect seem to distinguish educators who place learning first from those who do not.

The legitimacy of this perspective is evident when considering the challenges of students enrolled in a typical large, research-driven university without a learning-centered focus. College freshmen find themselves in classes with hundreds of other students. Professors are knowledge distributors in these introductory courses. It is the teacher's job to convey information and define expectations, and the student's job is to respond to the expectations and perform in a satisfactory manner.

Meanwhile, in sharp contrast to the freshman lecture course, the senior seminar is interactive and engaging. The professor serves as a guide, and the students are challenged to embark on an individualized learning journey that will open previously unimagined doors of opportunity.

Unlike their university colleagues, community college educators do not have the luxury of four years to move toward a learning-centered culture. Nor do they have the option of using introductory courses to screen students who might not possess the cognitive skills to complete a rigorous academic curriculum. Instead, students are accepted as they are; support programs and academic curricula create opportunities for students' development; and, as a result, learning environments develop that help students achieve more than they ever thought possible.

In *Servanthood: Leadership for the Third Millennium*, Sims suggests a servant mentality to facilitate a learning-centered culture because it "acknowledges and respects the freedom of another and seeks to enhance the other's capacity to make a difference" (p. x). In encouraging servanthood, Sims suggests a contemporary definition of the term, where servanthood becomes "a holistic approach that includes a genuine concern for individuals in their need for personal autonomy, as well as care for the social order in its need for compassion and justice"(p. 118).

A close parallel can be drawn between Sims' and Greenleaf's descriptions of servant leaders and the state of mind necessary to practice learning-centeredness. Both perspectives underscore the need to treat those served with respect and to develop their capacity to act autonomously. Both focus on a person's growth and development. And both strategies gauge their effectiveness by the impact of the interaction, not only on the person being served but also on the whole of society.

Just as O'Banion (1997) called for a new way of thinking and for placing students first, so do Sims and Greenleaf suggest a holistic approach to serving that reflects concern for students, respect for their personal autonomy, and awareness that what educators do in their lives affects the social order of the world. Servanthood presents the framework for practitioners to practice learning-centeredness. By approaching their work as servants, educators place students first and create conditions that foster student development.

The following servant attributes will contribute to a learning-centered college environment:

1. **Demonstrating respect and compassion for students.** A servant educator views all students with respect and looks for strengths to build upon rather than challenges that limit success.

2. **Empathic listening and direct communicating.** A servant educator listens more often than speaks, understands students' points of view, and uses this understanding to develop deep and lasting connections with students. Furthermore, empathic listening helps students to feel valued and worthwhile—conditions that increase the likelihood that they will persist through challenges and complete academic goals.

3. **Willingness to combine high degrees of challenge with adequate amounts of support.** Servant educators instill an image of what a student is capable of achieving and push students to work beyond their fears and perceived limitations. In addition, students are directed to assume responsibility for their learning. However, strong challenge accompanies a supportive environment, so the student can reach high without an overwhelming sense that failure is inevitable.

4. **Looking for compromise and opportunities for collaboration.** Servant educators are willing to compromise if it will lead to increased student achievement. The opportunity to support learning is more important than the need to be right. However, servant educators also know the limits of compromise and are quick to distinguish

between enabling a learner's poor decisions and yielding to a student's perspective because this compromise will foster student growth. In addition, a servant educator creates opportunities for collaboration throughout the college, knowing that "involving [students] in decision-making as a way of making wiser decisions radically changes the way one listens to others" (Sims, 1997, p. 89). Furthermore, willingness to collaborate and to yield control fosters student initiative, creativity, critical thinking, and independent action.

5. **Being courageous and acting on conviction.** Servant educators are confident in their skills and willing to go against the norm. They break away from those who encourage their conformity and hold true to their principles when criticized.

CONCLUSION

Neither institutional change nor moving colleges toward a learning-centered culture is easy. Barbara Brown Taylor defined the challenges of initiating change by saying, "It's enough to give you whiplash, trying to comfort the frightened traditionalists with one hand while reaching out to the enlightened seekers with the other. It would be a whole lot easier to ignore one group or the other . . . but, if you ask me, the stretch is an occupational hazard. It is just what one must do when you are living between the end of one world and the beginning of another" (Sims, 1997. p. 75).

Most proposed changes in colleges and universities, including moving from practitioner-directed to learning-centered interaction, become stymied or derailed by competing views. While the transition to a learning-centered philosophy may seem like the beginning of a new world, faculty and administrative discussion on the meaningfulness of the transition often limits its implementation. All too often, the enlightened seekers grow weary and yield to the frightened traditionalists.

How can a college overcome the obstacles presented by those who resist change? An important first step is to understand the nature of the resistance. Sims suggests that "resistance to change and the overcoming of change is not basically an institutional issue. It is personal. It only takes an institutional form because that is how individual persons relate to one another" (p. 84).

Margaret Wheatley offers a solution to overcoming resistance that should be obvious to the seasoned educator. Just as student development staff members engage their students in a learning experience, so too must change seekers involve those who resist in proposing solutions. No constituent group can be ignored.

While Sims and Wheatley encourage an inclusive approach, Sanford C. Shugart offers a hopeful solution to educators who find their real-life experiences far removed from the exemplary programs and best practices highlighted at conferences and professional training seminars. Looking back at the scenarios cited at the beginning of the chapter, Shugart suggests ways for Mario to demonstrate learning-centeredness even when there are more students needing counseling than he is capable of serving. Mario cannot rely on the institution to solve his dilemma, nor can he expect the organization to be responsive to his needs. After all, there is no money to increase staffing, no matter how drastic the need for the services. Rather, Mario will need to practice the five attributes of a servant educator. His professional training and experience prepare him in listening, communication, conflict resolution, and problem solving. While he won't serve all who need help, he can make a difference with those he assists. Mario will need strong conviction and courage to avoid trying to do too much, realizing that he must be fully engaged with his students to help them through their challenges, rather than seeing more students but spending too little time with anyone to make a difference. Perhaps Mario can broaden the net of support by training some academic faculty members or student leaders to address issues that don't require his level of professional skill. Whatever approach Mario chooses, he must be careful not to overload himself with an impossible challenge, for no one can help others if they don't take care of themselves.

Sara, on the other hand, will benefit from the direction offered by Sims and Wheatley. Sara must take time to understand the president's reasons for the administrative reorganization and find ways of blending her passion to develop connections to diverse students with the president's intentions. Expanding collaborations and forming partnerships will be necessary, since Sara no longer leads the team implementing the program. The new dean of counseling is an essential partner, but expanding the base of involvement as soon as possible will capture people's enthusiasm and energy. While no longer directly involved, Sara can still be a champion for student connectivity in the college and identify other people to pick up where she left off. If Sara remains courageous and continues to act on her convictions, she and others will create a better climate for learning.

Sara and Mario have learned that institutional limitations are not a deterrent to fostering student learning. Rather, both student affairs professionals understand that the power of personal conviction and vocational commitment is too strong to be restrained. Therefore, both are poised to move their college in a learning-centered direction.

REFERENCES

American College Personnel Association. (1994). *The student learning imperative: Implications for student affairs.* Alexandria, VA.

Greenleaf, R. K. (1991). *Servant leadership: A journey into the nature of legitimate power and greatness.* New York: Paulist Press.

Harvey-Smith, A. B. (2003). *The adoption of the learning paradigm in student affairs divisions in Vanguard community colleges.* Unpublished doctoral dissertation, University of Maryland, College Park.

National Association of Student Personnel Administrators. (1987). *A perspective on student affairs.* Washington, DC.

O'Banion, T. (1997). *A learning college for the 21st century.* Phoenix, AZ: Oryx Press.

Palmer, P. J. (1998). *The courage to teach: Exploring the inner landscape of a teacher's life.* San Francisco: Jossey-Bass.

Sims, B. J. (1997). *Servanthood: Leadership for the third millennium.* Cambridge, MA: Cowley Publications.

Study Group on the Condition of Excellence in American Higher Education. (1984). *Involvement in learning: Realizing the potential of American higher education.* Washington, DC: National Institute of Education.

It's All About Relationships

Susan Komives

"Change is the way the future invades our lives."

—ALVIN TOFFLER

If change is the way the future invades our lives as Toffler attests, then leadership is the way we invade the future. Taking charge of our shared future is a mandate for all professionals reading this book or any book like it. We cannot wait for the external pressures identified in these chapters to incite us to change but must marshal our collective energy and professionalism to move our campuses toward a successful, shared future. When we can see issues that must be addressed, we must think together and act. To do anything less may be unethical. Robert Greenleaf (1977) projected in *Servant Leadership* that in the future, our failure to foresee may even be viewed as an "ethical failure" because some of our problems today are actually the result of a failure "to make the effort at an earlier date to foresee today's events and take the right actions when there was freedom for initiative to act" (p. 26).

We might understand our challenges better if we admitted the heresy that higher educational institutions are not learning organizations (Woodard, Love, & Komives, 2000). Learning clearly happens in them, but we have largely been unsuccessful operating as an organization of people who know how to learn together to address our shared problems. This book's emphasis on learning how to be a learning organization and adopting a culture of learning is critical to the transformation of our organizations, and appears to be a lynchpin of the culture readiness promoted in the seventh learning college principle.

Adopting a learning college model is a complex campus change that involves all systems of the institution: human, political, structural, and symbolic (Bolman & Deal, 2003). ACE's studies (Eckel, Hill, & Green, 1998) on how change happens on campus identified two dimensions of change that categorize four kinds of change initiatives.

Figure 1: Transformative Change

Reproduced with permission of the American Council on Education from Eckel, P., Hill, B., & Green, M. (1998). *On Change I: En Route to Transformation.* Washington, DC: American Council on Education.

Depth

	Low	High
Low	Adjustment (I)	Isolated Change (II)
High	Far-Reaching Change (III)	Transformational Change (IV)

Pervasiveness

The pervasiveness and depth of transformative change involve the very culture of the organization. Readying that culture to engage in a transformation is essential to the process (Harvey-Smith, 2003).

In today's networked world, we know that we need to work together very differently than we usually do to accomplish transformative outcomes. Allen and Cherry (2000) frame this as new ways of leading, new ways of relating, new ways of changing, and new ways of learning together in our organizations. Although we exist in complex, hierarchical organizations, most institutions have come to rely on cross-functional processes to address our complex problems. There is great hope in these practices because they model being a learning organization and they bring good thinking from diverse perspectives to these issues instead of perpetuating siloed thinking that created many of our problems (Komives, 1996). Further, these collaborative relationships across the institution shape the culture to learn to trust and depend on each other. It is absolutely essential to nurture healthy relationships in the institution.

The systemic, transformative change called for in every chapter of this book requires "rethinking" student affairs work (Love & Estanek, 2004) to embrace the paradoxes that are so essential in transformative work. It is a paradox that change requires stability, yet busy human beings in work environments need predictable dimensions of their lives that have comfortable continuity to truly be able to do the hard mental work of thinking anew about change. Adopting a learning college model requires a culture of collaboration. It is a paradox that collaboration is built on individual action and initiative (Woodard, Love, & Komives, 2000). Individuals need to step up and say, "Yes, I will join with you in this shared activity" or "We can do this together." This collaboration recognizes that: "Relationships are the connective tissue of the organization . . . over time, these new relationships, built on trust and integrity, become the glue that holds us together" (Allen & Cherrey, 2000, p. 31). Individuals need to overcome any resistance and trust the process of the journey the organization is to undertake. This happens best in a culture where trust and care prevail and where risk is encouraged. *Leadership Reconsidered: Engaging Higher Education in Social Change* (Astin & Astin, 2000) identifies the dynamic reciprocity between individual qualities and group qualities so essential in new ways of relating and leading to a collaborative culture in today's higher education culture (see Figure 2).

Figure 2

Leadership Reconsidered: Engaging Higher Education in Social Change, Astin & Astin, 2000

What is Effective Leadership?	
Group Qualities	Individual Qualities
Shared purpose—reflects the shared aims and values of the group's members; can take time to achieve	*Commitment*—the passion, intensity, and persistence that supplies energy, motivates individuals, and drives group effort
Collaboration—an approach that empowers individuals, engenders trust, and capitalizes on diverse talents	*Empathy*—the capacity to put yourself in another's place; requires the cultivation and use of listening skills
Division of labor—requires each member of the group to make a significant contribution to the overall effort	*Competence*—the knowledge, skill, and technical expertise required for successful completion of the transformation effort
Disagreement with respect—recognizes that disagreements are inevitable and should be handled in an atmosphere of mutual trust	*Authenticity*—consistency between one's actions and one's most deeply felt values and beliefs
A learning environment—allows members to see the group as a place where they can learn and acquire skills	*Self-knowledge*—awareness of the beliefs, values, attitudes, and emotions that motivate one to seek change

Transforming our institutions into student-centered learning colleges is a big challenge. Echoing Terry O'Banion's theme in the Foreword, in the student-centered learning college, all campus educators are responsible for student learning outcomes. ACPA and NASPA have recently released a thoughtful agenda for our future, *Learning Reconsidered: A Campus-Wide Focus on the Student Experience* (2004). This monograph says that student learning is the complex integration of academic learning with personal development and identity. Learning and development are not to be thought of as different sides of the same coin but as the same side of the coin. This kind of learning happens all across the environment. *Learning Reconsidered* asserts that all campus educators need to be held accountable for student learning outcomes, and that all resources of the institution should work together to promote those outcomes.

This kind of institutional transformation is built on individual transformation. It starts with each of us. We must be learners, willing to say we do not know how to make this happen but willing to try. We must be civically engaged in our institutions—seeing ourselves as responsible members of our campus communities as well as responsible members of our division. We must claim our educational role—knowing how our programs and services educate students and support their college success.

The final paradox we must address is how can we create student-centered learning colleges and not create processes that engage students as change agent partners in this journey? We too often leave students out of the process. We must rethink all of our processes and put students at the center of the change initiatives as full partners and key stakeholders. We continue to do things *to* students and *for* students. We need to rethink the educational process and do things *with* students and expect students to do things for themselves (Komives, 1994). Students will learn best when they are expected to be civically engaged members of our communities sharing in this transformation.

A personal note

The image of doing a dissertation engenders many images for those contemplating the process, starting the process, being bogged down in the process, or having successfully finished the process. The best outcomes come from learners who are passionate about their topic, see a clear contribution to practice, and are truly eager to learn from every new pathway the study reveals. Alicia was that learner, and her good work in her dissertation is revealed in the further work of herself and her authors in each of these chapters. As her co-traveler in this journey (a.k.a. her adviser), it was a pleasure to be a co-meaning maker and learn from her study. May the same happen for any reader of this book who is considering a dissertation.

REFERENCES

Allen, K. E., & Cherrey, C. (2000). *Systemic leadership: Enriching the meaning of our work.* Washington, DC: American College Personnel Association and National Association of Campus Activities.

American College Personnel Association and National Association of Student Personnel Administrators. (2004). *Learning reconsidered: A campus-wide focus on the student experience.* Washington, DC: American College Personnel Association and National Association.

Astin, A. W., & Astin, H. S. (Eds.). (2000). *Leadership reconsidered: Engaging higher education in social change.* Battle Creek, MI: W. K. Kellogg Foundation.

Bolman, L. G., & Deal, T. E. (2003). *Reframing organizations: Artistry, choice, and leadership* (3rd ed.). San Francisco: Jossey-Bass.

Eckel, P., Hill, B., & Green, M. (1998). *On change I: En route to transformation.* Washington, DC: American Council on Education.

Greenleaf, R. (1977). *Servant leadership.* Mahwah, NJ: Paulist Press.

Harvey-Smith, A. B. (2003). *The adoption of the learning paradigm in student affairs divisions in Vanguard community colleges.* Unpublished doctoral dissertation, University of Maryland, College Park.

Komives, S. R. (1994). Increasing student involvement through civic leadership education. In C. C. Schroeder & P. Mable (Eds.), *Realizing the educational potential of college residence halls* (pp. 218-240). San Francisco: Jossey-Bass.

Komives, S. R. (1996). A call to collaborative leadership. *About Campus, 1*(3), 2-3.

Love, P. G., & Estanek, S. M. (2004). *Rethinking student affairs practice.* San Francisco: Jossey-Bass.

Woodard, D. B., Jr., Love, P., & Komives, S. R. (2000). *Leadership and management issues for a new century* (New Directions for Student Services, No. 92). San Francisco: Jossey-Bass.

Interdisciplinary Reaction: Critical Influences On Change

Rufus Sylvester Lynch and Jacquelyn Mitchell

"When the music changes, so does the dance."

—WEST AFRICAN PROVERB

INTRODUCTION

Change in education is not new. The history of higher education is replete with change initiatives. There have been recurring calls for change, often in the form of "dazzling new experiments" and "dazzling innovations" that attempt to insure educational effectiveness (Boyer, 1996, p. 20).

Multidimensional change in higher education has involved both the internal and external environments of the academy. Reform agendas have addressed issues as diverse as academic programs, the role of the professorate, student issues, governance, and community partnerships. Each initiative is precipitated by changes in the social environment (Boyer, 1990; Gumport, 2001; Rudolph, 1977).

As is true for earlier periods of reform, the "dance" of change in the academy reflects an evolution in societal perspectives. However, the social environment of the 21st century appears to be more complex than that of earlier periods, and the demands placed on colleges and universities are challenging, costly, and sometimes incompatible (Gumport, 2001). Economic turbulence and retrenchment, technological revolution, population diversity, workforce transitions, mandated outcomes, and litigiousness are among the challenges. The educational organization is challenged to thrive and to maintain its institutional integrity and mission within this conundrum (Eckel, Hill, & Green, 1998; Kezar, 2001).

This appendix focuses on selected influences on change efforts, which should be taken into account if authentic transformation is to be achieved.

The literature documents several influences on successful change initiatives. The need for an increased awareness and a heightened response to change was suggested by Banathy, who described the current response of institutions of higher learning to change in this fashion: "the ship of education may be on troubled waters, with its crew attempting isolated, piecemeal efforts to repair individual components rather than changing course to avoid the icebergs ahead" (1994, p. 17).

The elements of leadership, communication, institutional support, organizational culture, and institutionalization were found to be key in guiding the ship to successful organizational change (Artis, 1980; Cochren, 1995; Conner & Patterson, 1982; Curry, 1992; Frank & Rock, 1996; Harvey-Smith, 2003; Vortruba, 1983). What follows is a brief discussion of these elements and their importance to successful change in general and to the work in student affairs specifically, and an interdisciplinary reaction to the change taking shape in the academy through the lens of social work and law.

Leadership is a central element in effecting intentional organizational change and essential in providing a foundation for successful change. Ely (1990) identified it as one of the eight conditions of change.

Communication is vital to initiating and sustaining change. Student affairs divisions must create and maintain an institution-wide system of communication and feedback to achieve success.

Organizations are encouraged to identify and provide appropriate institutional support to launch and sustain change. Student affairs divisions are encouraged to support organizational efforts through changes in structure, adoption of initiatives, evaluation of outcomes, and hiring personnel who fit the shift in paradigms.

The organization's culture provides a vehicle through which members of the community make meaning of the changes taking place. Schein

(1992) posited that cultures also influence community members' receptivity to change and how experiences are viewed and evaluated.

Student affairs divisions can play a crucial role in effectively managing the complexity of change through transforming cultures in support of successful change in their unique environments and aiding in creating cultures that are more open and responsive to change and learning as indicated by the seventh learning college principle (Harvey-Smith, 2003). Cultural transformations should involve support for a seamless relationship between academic affairs and student affairs, encouraging a comprehensive model of collaboration.

The integration or institutionalization of change initiatives has significant impact on the long-term success and sustainability of change. Curry (1992) cited institutionalization as one of the three necessary steps in implementing change. Harvey-Smith defined institutionalization in her 2003 study as the point at which institutional changes become part of the culture and are considered regular practice.

ORGANIZATIONAL SYNERGY

Colleges and universities are organizations formed for the purpose of carrying out a particular enterprise (Broom & Selznick, 1963) "and respond like other large organizations to the need for change in similar ways" (Van Loon, 2001, p. 297).

The notion of the educational institution as a "learning organization" is based on a concept introduced by Senge (1990) and reflects the systemic nature of colleges and universities. Learning organizations are said to have "enhanced capacity to learn, adapt, and change" and "vision, strategy, values, structure, systems, processes, and practices" that work collectively to foster individual development and accelerate systemic learning (Gephart, Marsick, Van Buren, & Spiro, 1996, pp. 36, 38).

The exploration of the influences on change includes an assumption that educational institutions are complex systemic organizations that coexist. In addition to being affected by the factors within the environment, educational institutions help to shape the environment with which they contend.

The course of change is defined by the change theory or model selected to guide the process. The varied theories and models of change that have been advanced to drive and/or assess change processes in the academy are designed to respond to synergistic challenges (Kezar, 2001; Rogers, 1995; Scott, 2001) but have been unevenly embraced (El-Khawas, 2002; Levine, 1980).

To further explore the influence of the framework selected on the change process, the discussion moves further in a transdisciplinary direction, incorporating the discipline of social work and law as a conceptual base.

PROBLEM SOLVING: A SYNERGISTIC CHANGE PROCESS

Helen Perlman (1957) is credited with introducing the concept of problem solving into the social work lexis, adapting the work of theorists such as John Dewey. Based on the scientific method, "problem solving" is but one professional process (Cohen & Nagel, 1934; Stone, 1978). It is a planned, deductive approach to change intervention that accommodates multidisciplinary use, providing a process framework for a variety of professional applications, including social work practice, the scientific method, real estate appraisals, counseling, and education (Cohen & Nagel, 1934; Compton & Galaway, 1999; Mundy, 1992).

The scientific method is a process through which knowledge is generated, via potentially recurring steps in flexible order: 1) problem recognition; 2) hypothesis; 3) inquiry design; 4) design implementation; and 5) analysis/interpretation.

Over the years, problem solving evolved in the social work literature. We suggest conceptually extending the basic problem-solving framework through a concentric "wheel" to emphasize the nonlinear nature of the process. The model includes six phases: 1) agenda engagement, 2) problem definition, 3) plan development, 4) plan finalization, 5) implementation, and 6) evaluation.

The process is not statically sequential. Each phase influences all other phases. The process embraces the social reality, including the synergistic responses of all systems interdependent with the educational institution. At the same time, the problem-solving process offers guideposts for the change process and stakeholders (Compton & Galaway, 1999, p. 90).

Agenda Engagement

The decision to make a change is a significant driver of the process. The literature is replete with discussion of the external pressures for change that are faced by educational institutions. External pressures are significant stimuli for the initiation of change agendas in colleges and universities. Moreover, each of these changes in the educational institution may also precipitate other changes, often as unintended consequences (Compton & Galaway, 1999; Edwards, 1999; Kezar & Eckel, 2002). For example, changes mandated by budgetary woes often precipitate changes in tuition rates, personnel complements, and allocations for general and educational expenses.

The decision to engage change has repercussions within the educational institution as well as externally. Consequently, the change effort is most often colored by the extent to which potentially affected internal and external stakeholders support the proposed change. Kezar and Eckel (2002) have observed:

> Transformational change is unfamiliar to most higher education institutions; it (a) alters the culture of the institution by changing select underlying assumptions and institutional behaviors, processes, and products; (b) is deep and pervasive, affecting the whole institution; (c) is intentional; and (d) occurs over time. (pp. 295-296)

Problem Definition

This is a crucial phase of any change agenda and significantly colors the change process. How the problem is defined essentially drives the change process and is subject to revision throughout the change process (Locke, Garrison, & Winship, 1998). The accuracy with which the problem is analyzed and defined influences the outcome of a change process and may lead to a decision not to attempt the transformation.

Plan Development

The recurring issue associated with this phase is determination of possible change strategies and the benefits and disadvantages of each, given the problem definition. For example, the decision to adopt plans to implement efficiency measures, in response to societal pressures, has had unintended effects in educational institutions, including reductions in academic offerings, tuition increases, and professorial resources (Gumport, 2000). Thus, a change agenda to reduce the operational scale of a college or university should be accompanied by attention to the potential of supplemental agenda to address recurring repercussions in other parts of the system.

Plan Finalization

The final decision to adopt a strategy or plan offers another opportunity to abort the change agenda, make revisions to the problem definition, or identify new change agendas.

Mojab and Gorman (2003) offer an example of the influence of the benefits and disadvantages of plans adopted by educational institutions to change to "learning organizations." The plan for action should be specific enough to accomplish the objectives, to address the problem as defined (Compton & Galaway, 1999), and to accommodate ecological issues, growth status, learning, and human environment dynamics, as appropriate.

Implementation

Several dynamics shape implementation of the change process. The literature chronicles a variety of change implementation experiences in educational institutions. ACE's "En Route to Transformation" monograph (Eckel, Hill, & Green, 1998) explored the change implementation experiences of

26 colleges and universities. The examination concluded with a significant "unanswered question" relative to the implementation process: What are the most successful circumstantial strategies?

Evaluation

Through evaluation, methods are used to measure the change process and the outcomes of that process. Moreover, evaluation is to be distinguished from monitoring of the process or the recurring scanning within the process (Compton & Galaway, 1999).

The evaluation should be designed to focus on the extent to which the plan, as implemented, responded to the problem defined for the change agenda.

SYNERGY BETWEEN THE LAW AND THE ACADEMY

This final section addresses the influence on the change process of the law. Three major themes recur in an exploration of the influence of the law on change processes in the academy: 1) both the law and education are social institutions that are, necessarily, in continuous synergy; 2) the pervasiveness of the law; and 3) the preference for legal dispute resolution. Indeed, these themes reflect critical pivot points in any change process, defining what change may be pursued and the manner in which it may be accomplished (Lynch & Mitchell, 1995b).

The law is:

> a collection of rules of social control derived from various constitutions, statutes, regulations and case law. The law is the written standards, principles, processes and rules that are adopted, administered, and enforced by a government entity that regulates behavior by setting forth what people may do and how they may do it. (Lynch & Mitchell, 1995b, p. 10)

Education and the law are mutually influential. The synergy between the two institutions reaches into subsystems in each institution. Any change agenda is highly dependent on these dynamics.

The Broad Reach of the Law

At least since the 1960s, a plethora of mandates has invaded the "halls of ivy" (Edelman, 1990; Mitchell & Lynch, 1997). Colleges and universities must daily balance the interests of various stakeholders that are often embedded in employment laws, civil rights laws, tort laws, accreditation standards, patent laws, constitutional rights, tax law, and international law.

Similarly, the business of education generates issues and circumstances that trigger vital legal issues (Selznick, 2003). The literature contains a panoply of exemplars, including the imposition of statutory protections for students, faculty, and staff such as the Americans with Disabilities Act of 1990; affirmative action laws; and other antidiscrimination measures that may be viewed as placing added responsibilities on the academy.

The litigiousness of American society is widely known. In the academy, the legal rights and responsibilities of stakeholders color change processes. Academic decisions on student performance are now proscribed by legal principles such as due process. As a result, educational institutions are faced with revising policies in response to adverse rulings or making changes to avoid such consequences. In both instances, legal principles frame the change agenda (Makar, 2002; Rochford, 2001).

The law-education synergy is clearly visible inside the academy, in the legal environment and in society generally. This synergy precipitates and emanates change in the academy, the legal environment and in society. (Johnson & Duffett, 2003; Grutter v. Bolinger, 2003; Rochford, 2001; Thomas, 2000)

The Law and Change: Implications for the Academy

Although the tendency is to lament the dramatic impact of the law and legal processes on the academy, the influence is actually bi-directional. Both the law and education influence each other and are consistently influenced by each other, and both affect the social landscape. The law is a pervasive dynamic in all of society and has emerged as the preferred method of dispute resolution.

Given these realities, the academy must have the resources to thrive in a social context that is significantly defined by legalistic mandates. Preparedness for maintaining the institutional integrity of the academy while navigating future challenges requires "legal literacy." Borrowing from social work, the development of legal literacy would include the following requisites:

1. Knowledge of the law, legal processes, and procedures that affect the academy

2. Inclusion of content on law, legal processes, and legal procedures in educational curricula, continuing education, conferences, and on-the-job training

3. Development of education leadership resources that include content on the law, legal processes, and legal procedures

4. Expansion of the attention of professional associations to content on law, legal processes, and legal procedures (Mitchell, 2002).

Models for the inclusion of legal literacy content have been developed for other nonlegal professions (see, e.g., Kopels & Gustavsson, 1996; Lynch & Mitchell, 1995a) that might provide guidance for the academy. The models ultimately developed can be determined through the exercise of the collective wisdom of all institutional stakeholders, both internal and external. The development of such literacy is at least one key to preservation of the academy as a major social institution with its mission preserved.

We are not proposing the transformation of educators into lawyers. We are simply encouraging educators to acquire the literacy that would facilitate awareness of the legal pitfalls of change agenda and to seek the input of legal professionals in a timely way.

CONCLUSION

In the future, educational institutions will, most probably, face even greater challenges to transforming. Therefore, awareness of the consequential and antecedent influences on change processes is essential.

We have proposed that three influences—the academy as an organization and social institution, the selected change process, and the law—have currency and will remain salient in future change processes. The success of the academy in rechoreographing to maintain its vitality and relevance is pivotal for the social institution of education. Perhaps most important as we move forward with transformations, we should be mindful of the pivotal societal role and potential influence of education. As Thomas Jefferson counseled, an educated electorate is essential to a democratic society.

REFERENCES

Artis, J. B. (1980). An ethnographic case study of the administrative organization, processes, and behavior in a selected senior high school. (Doctoral dissertation, University of Wisconsin, 1980). *Dissertation Abstracts International, 101,* 123-135.

Banathy, B. (1994). Designing educational systems: Creating our future in a changing world. In C. Reigeluth & R. Garfinkle (Eds.), *Systemic change in education* (pp. 27-34). Englewood Cliffs, NJ: Sage Publications.

Boyer, E. L. (1990). Scholarship reconsidered: Priorities of the professoriate. *Issues in Accounting Education, 7*(1), 87-91.

Boyer, E. L. (1996). An idea that people share. *Independent School, 55*(2), 20-29.

Broom, L., & Selznick, P. (1963). *Sociology: A text with adapted readings* (3rd ed.). New York: Harper & Row.

Cochren, J. R. (1995). *Leadership in an era of retrenchment.* (ERIC Document Reproduction Service No. ED 387 905).

Cohen, M., & Nagel, E. (1934). *An introduction to logic and the scientific method.* New York: Harcourt Brace Jovanovich Harper & Row.

Compton, B. R., & Galaway, B. (1999). *Social work processes* (6th ed.). Pacific Grove, CA: Brooks/Cole Publishing Co.

Conner, D., & Patterson, R. (1982). Building commitment to organizational change. *Training and Development Journal, 36*(4), 18-26.

Curry, B. K. (1992). *Instituting enduring innovations: Achieving continuity of change in higher education* (Report No. EDO-HE-92-7). Washington, DC: Office of Education Research and Improvement. (ERIC Document Reproduction Service No. ED 358 811).

Eckel, P., Hill, B., & Green, M. (1998). *On change: En route to transformation.* Washington, DC: American Council on Education.

Edelman, L. B. (1990). Legal environments and organizational governance: The expansion of due process in the American workplace. *American Journal of Sociology, 95*(6), 1401-1440.

Edwards, R. (1999). The academic department: How does it fit into the university reform agenda? *Change, 31*(5), 17-27.

El-Khawas, E. (2002). Reform initiatives in higher education (Report No. EDO-HE-2002-10). Washington, DC: Office of Educational Research and Improvement. (ERIC Document Reproduction Service No. ED 470 037).

Ely, D. (1990). Conditions that facilitate the implementation of educational technology innovations. *Journal of Research on Computing in Education, 23,* 298-305.

Frank, D., & Rock, W. (1996). *Exploiting instability: A model for managing organizational change.* Phoenix, AZ: Proceedings of the annual international conference of the National Community College Chair Academy.

Gephart, M. A., Marsick, V. J., Van Buren, M. E., & Spiro, M. S. (1996). Learning organizations come alive. *Training & Development, 50*(12), 34-45.

Grutter v. Bolinger, 123 S. Ct. 2325 (2003).

Gumport, P. J. (2001). Restructuring: imperatives and opportunities for academic leaders. *Innovative Higher Education, 25*(4), 239-251.

Gumport, P. J. (2000). Academic restructuring: Organizational change and institutional imperatives. *Higher Education,* 39, 67-91.

Harvey-Smith, A. B. (2003). *The adoption of the learning paradigm in student affairs divisions in Vanguard Community Colleges.* Unpublished doctoral dissertation, University of Maryland, College Park.

Isaacson, N. & Bamburg, J. (1992). Can schools become learning organizations? *Educational Leadership, 50*(3), 42-44.

Johnson, J., & Duffett, A. (2003). *"I'm calling my lawyer": How litigation, due process and other regulatory requirements are affecting public education.* New York: Public Agenda.

Kezar, A. (2001). Understanding and facilitating change in higher education in the 21st century (Report No. EDO-HE-2001-07). Washington, DC: Office of Educational Research and Improvement. (ERIC Document Reproduction Service No. ED 457 763).

Kezar, A., & Eckel, P. (2002). Examining the institutional transformation process: The importance of sensemaking, interrelated strategies, and balance. *Research in Higher Education, 43*(3), 295-328.

Kopels, S., & Gustavsson, N. S. (1996). Infusing legal issues into the social work curricula. *Journal of Social Work Education, 32*(1), 115-125.

Levine, A. (1980). *Why innovation fails.* Albany, NY: SUNY Press.

Locke, B., Garrison, R., & Winship, J. (1998). *Generalist social work practice: Context, story, and partnerships.* Pacific Grove, CA: Brooks/Cole.

Lynch, R. S., & Mitchell, J. (1995a). Judicial social worker practice model: Paradigm for a specialty and curricula enhancement. *Journal of Law and Social Work, 5*(1), 25-40.

Lynch, R. S., & Mitchell, J. (1995b). Justice system advocacy: A must for NASW and the social work community. *Social Work, 40*(1), 9-12.

Makar, S. D. (2002, November 8). Litigious students and academic disputes. *Chronicle of Higher Education, 49*(11), B20.

Mitchell, J. (2002). Is social work Y2K compliant? Adapting to the mandates of future practice. In I. A. Neighbors, A. Chambers, E. Levin, G. Nordman, & C. Tutrone (Eds.), *Social work and the law: Proceedings of the National Organization of Forensic Social Work,* 2000 (pp. 59-77).

Mitchell, J., & Lynch, R.S. (1997). Do the ethical standards of the profession carry a higher authority than the law? No. In E. Gambrill & R. Pruger (Eds.), *Controversial issues in social work ethics, values, and obligations* (pp. 131-135). Boston: Allyn & Bacon.

Mojab, S., & Gorman, R. (2003). Women and consciousness in the "learning organization": Emancipation or exploitation. *Adult Education Quarterly, 53*(4), 228-242.

Mundy, B. (1992). The scientific method and the appraisal process. *Appraisal Journal, 60*(4), 493-499.

Perlman, H. H. (1957). *Social casework.* Chicago: University of Chicago Press.

Rochford, F. (2001). Issues of university governance and management giving rise to legal liability. *Journal of Higher Education Policy and Management, 23*(1), 49- 61.

Rogers, E. (1995). *Diffusion of innovations* (4th ed.). New York: Free Press.

Rudolph, F. (1977). *Curriculum: A history of the American undergraduate course of study since 1636.* San Francisco: Jossey-Bass.

Schein, E. H. (1992). *Organizational culture in leadership* (2nd ed.). San Francisco: Jossey-Bass.

Selznick, P. (2003). "Law in context" revisited. *Journal of Law and Society, 30*(2), 177-186.

Senge, P. (1990). *The fifth discipline.* New York: Doubleday.

Scott, W. R. (2001). *Institutions and organizations* (2nd ed.). Thousand Oaks, CA: Sage.

Stone, E. F. (1978). Research method in organizational behavior. Glenview, IL: Scott, Foresman.

Thomas, S. B. (2000). College students and disability law. *Journal of Special Education, 33*(4), 248-257.

Van Loon, R. (2001). Organizational change: A case study. *Innovative Higher Education, 25*(4), 285-301.

Vortruba, J. C. (1983, April). *Evaluating organizational change strategies for university continuing education.* Paper presented at the annual meeting of the American Educational Research Association, Montreal, Quebec, Canada.